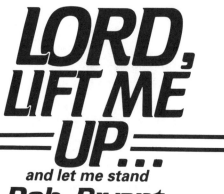

LORD, LIFT ME UP...
and let me stand
—Rob Bryant—

BROADMAN PRESS
NASHVILLE, TENNESSEE

To my wife Wanice
and my children Jason and Jonathan

© Copyright 1990 ● Broadman Press
All rights reserved
4250-87
ISBN: 0-8054-5087-4
Dewey Decimal Classification: B
Subject Heading: BRYANT, ROB // PHYSICALLY HANDICAPPED - BIOGRAPHY
Library of Congress Catalog Number: 89-38429
Printed in the United States of America

Library of Congress Cataloging-in-Publication Data

Bryant, Rob, 1955-
    Lord, lift me up-- / Rob Bryant.
      p. cm.
    Summary: Rob Bryant, an active Christian, recounts his life before and after his conversion, his transformation from a smart-aleck military man who violated security regulations to a caring and responsible individual, and his accident which left him a paraplegic.
    ISBN: 0-8054-5087-4
    1. Bryant, Rob, 1955- . 2. Christian biography--United States.
3. Paraplegics--United States--Biography. [1. Bryant, Rob, 1955-
. 2. Paraplegics. 3. Physically handicapped. 4. Christian Life.]
I. Title.
BR1725.B72A3 1990
248.8'6'092--dc20
[B]

                [92] 89-38429
                       CIP
                       AC

Contents

1
The Long Night

"Seek, Boy," I whispered to my patrol dog.

He charged out to the end of the leash, sniffed the air, and slowly scanned the horizon. My canine friend, a ninety-pound German Shepherd, was trained and ready to attack. First, he would have to track down his prey.

Appropriately enough, his name was Satan. We began walking north, parallel to the lake near the end of my post. The road seemed clear, but I wanted to make sure. As we passed the first security bunker, we paused quietly to be certain we were alone. Satan lifted his nose and tested the air, methodically turning his head to the right and then to the left.

Once he was satisfied we were alone, he panted with a seeming smile on his face. As I started walking again, Satan kept up his alert scanning.

Each bunker was buried inside a man-made hill so the earth formed an additional barrier to attack or entry. Only a metal garage-type door was visible. We stopped in front of the second bunker and repeated the same ritual we had performed hundreds of times before.

As we moved out again, the leash and Satan were like an extension of my arm, almost moving as part of my own body. After years of training, he was one of Air Force Security's "top dogs." With a nose over 1,000 times more sensitive than a man's and eyes able to detect the slightest movement from incredible distances, Satan was programmed to seek for intruders. I stopped at the last bunker and peered beyond all the fences and across the flight line.

Although my post was dark, the runways, alert area, and top security areas were lit up almost as bright as day. There was no sign of an interloper, and I could tell by Satan's calmness that he agreed no one was around. After he completed his surveillance of the area, he pivoted and returned to me.

"Seek, Boy," I repeated.

Satan was again out at the end of the leash. The area sergeant and the flight officer had already made their rounds, so we were probably alone. We headed south, the same direction from which we had just come.

From the top of a bunker, we surveyed the whole area. The lake spread out in front of us. The darkness overcame the light at about a hundred yards out. I wondered if anyone was staring back at us from the edge of the darkness. I thought, *Good grief, with my area lit up like midday, I'm a sitting-duck target!*

My worst apprehension was terrorist groups. They would give almost anything to obtain a nuclear weapon. If I were successful in my secret mission tonight, I was convinced that terrorist groups would have a harder time. My mind drifted back to many conversations with my various supervisors when we discussed the seeming lack of security at our weapon storage sites.

I had told them in graphic detail how an inside job could be pulled off. Many of the security troops had complained that they could not adequately protect the off-base site from attack, if and when such might occur. At the off-base site, only inert weapons were stored, yet the Air Force had trained thousands of men over the years to upgrade these weapons from inert to active, volatile instruments of destruction.

In the event of an assault and theft, there were plenty of persons around the world who could prepare a bomb to explode. If an outside force were to learn of the weaknesses I had described to my superiors, they could either buy off a guard to help them, or even try to pull it off themselves.

Maybe a guard would only be required not to sound the alarm as the actual theft were carried out. I was advised by my superiors to quit asking questions about security. So, I had developed a plan to demonstrate on a small scale what could be done on a grand scale with the proper manpower. I felt Security was growing lax.

I calculated I had five minutes in which to cover this ground, do what I intended, and leave undetected. I arrived at the small-arms building within two minutes. I took a furtive look toward the area supervisor's gate house. All seemed normally quiet. His truck was still parked by the security shack. I removed the leash from my hand as Satan watched me curiously. I pulled my M-16 gun strap over my head and leaned it up against the wall.

"OK, Boy, here goes."

Satan sensed my tension and looked at me strangely.

"It'll all be over in a minute, Old Buddy."

He started panting, but he seemed calm. I knew if I remained unruffled, he would also. *Keep cool, Rob. Don't get edgy. If you do, Satan will sense it. If you start acting overly nervous, he'll get jumpy.* He was trained to react to my moods. *To him, my showing nervousness could mean I was under duress and needed his help. He might attack someone if they walk up, and I happen not to be here to control him. Not only that, someone could be* seriously injured, *and then my address could be Leavenworth for quite a chunk of my life.* "Stay, Satan," I said, snapping out of my troubled thoughts.

He sat down obediently and remained alert. I figured I had three more minutes to get in and out before anyone could approach. I was convinced if I started my ploy I could finish it. In my mind I weighed the risks one more time. Were the dire possibilities worth making my point about lackadaisical security?

First, I encountered an entrance about the size of a single-car garage door. It moved up about six inches. I pushed in with my 200-pound frame, and the door gave way enough for me to squeeze through. The door slammed shut behind me. I cringed momentarily but then realized if someone were close enough to hear the noise, I was in trouble anyway. I remained motionless, waiting for my eyes to adjust to the dark room. I was keenly aware that as I stood there precious seconds were ticking away.

With an estimated two-and-one-half minutes to go, I moved straight ahead to a box of live ammunition. I still could not believe that this much live ammo was simply sitting in a tin shed, begging to be stolen. I opened the box, grabbed several handfuls of the .50-caliber rounds, and stuffed my pockets. This was a slow process, since the rounds were linked together and I had to roll them up to cram them into my pockets. Each round was approximately six inches long and was awkward to handle.

After loading myself down with bullets, I moved toward the door. Suddenly, the entire room lit up, and I was temporarily blinded by the intense light. As quickly as the light had come it was gone. I was so startled I couldn't move. My eyes slowly adjusted to the darkness once again, and I checked my watch. *Oh, good grief, I've been in the building over five minutes. I gotta get out of here!* I mumbled to myself.

Then I heard a noise. It started as a low rumble, which slowly grew louder until I realized all too well what it was—the area sergeant's truck. I looked toward the window. His truck lights were shining into the window as he rounded the end of my post. My foot tripped on something on the floor, causing me to fall forward. As I caught myself with my arms, a sick feeling swept over me. The noise was becoming louder as I rushed toward the door. The truck was now passing the building.

Oh, Lord, I hope my dog is still somewhere nearby. If the rascal's chasing that truck or running around, I'm sunk. The area sergeant will radio Command Security Control, and this place will be crawling with police and investigators. I'll have some real explaining to do from the wrong side of the bars! It's amazing how quickly your life flashes in front of you when trouble beckons. Finally balanced and back on my feet, I jerked the door toward me with so much force it almost jumped off its track. I squeezed through, and I couldn't believe what was before my eyes. Satan was sitting exactly where I had left him. He was looking up at me as if he had not even seen the truck go by. He was so placid I wondered if a truck had passed by at all. I looked up just in time to see the truck tail lights disappear around the corner.

Whew, I barely made it, I sighed in relief.

Baltic, the area sergeant, was at the other end of my post by now. So he would be turning around and coming back in only a few seconds. I picked up my leash and moved away from the building. That nauseous feeling coursed through me again. *What if he has seen Satan and has kept going looking for me? If I were in his shoes, I wouldn't get out of the truck to look for a K-9 handler with his dog just sitting there watching. He could be putting in a distress call right now. Even if he didn't see Satan, where am I going to tell the sergeant I was? He'll ask why I hadn't stopped him in the challenge position and asked him for the code of the evening.*

The end of my post was lit up as the truck started back toward me. I sought cover behind a bunker, as I had been trained. The theory was that I could see the oncoming person or truck, but they couldn't see me. In this way, I was in control of the situation and could release my dog or fire my weapon, if need be, to protect myself or my post.

I reached for my M-16. It was gone! I had left it beside the ammo shack. Now my heart was beating like a jackhammer. I couldn't challenge him without a weapon in my hands.

"Dear God, help me," I moaned under my breath.

What should I do? I have to challenge him.

Here goes, Rob, I sure hope they serve good food in the slammer.

Satan sensed I was unusually tense. Pulling hard on the leash, he wanted to attack whatever or whoever was causing me so much stress. Now the truck was only ten feet in front of me. I had let the vehicle come too close.

"Halt, who goes there?" I yelled.

The truck screeched to a stop, and Satan lunged forward, growling and baring his teeth. The force pulled me forward onto my hands and knees. Some of the ammo in my pockets fell out.

Well, that's it! I wailed to myself.

"Sergeant Baltic," came a brusque reply.

"Code Word?" I asked, trying to sound cool and collected. I pulled Satan back and soothed him.

"Yellow Rose," the sergeant shouted back.

"Come forward and be recognized," I demanded. The truck pulled slowly ahead until I could clearly see it was Baltic. I stood up and walked to the side of the road.

Now, I thought, *he'll pull up, ask me where my gun is, and then he'll ask me where I've been!*

I still wondered if the sergeant had sounded the alarm. Baltic pulled up beside me. His stern expression verified my fears.

"Where in the blazes were you, Bryant?"

"My dog alerted on something over by the fence. By the time I got back you were already past me," I blurted out.

Satan was still growling at the sergeant. Baltic's eyes relayed his suspicion that all was not right—but also that he couldn't quite figure it out.

"Well, stay on your toes, Bryant," he spoke roughly. "And control your dog, will you?"

The sergeant pondered the situation. It seemed he wanted to forget the entire incident. He was lingering, and I wanted to get rid of him before he noticed my M-16 was missing. How he had failed to notice I had no idea. A patrol dog handler without a gun is like a baseball player without a glove.

He started talking about his wife and kids. Then he went on about the flight officer and the security measures he was planning to put into effect. Suddenly, he realized he was doing a monologue.

"What's wrong with you, Bryant? You always have something to say."

"Aw, nothing, I just have a lot on my mind lately."

"Like what? Maybe I can help," he came back somewhat sarcastically, I thought.

"You know, just being single and away from home and . . ."

What a dumb thing to say, I thought, as I trailed off. Sergeant Baltic knew I enjoyed wild parties and having several girl friends at a time. I was never bored.

"Man, I wish I was single and away from home. If I was your age and single, I wouldn't have any problems. You'll see, someday when you're old and married, you'll wish you . . ."

"What time is it getting to be, Sarge?" I hoped to move him on his way. His tightened lips belied his disapproval at being interrupted, but he checked his watch.

"Our relief ought to be here in a few minutes. You want a ride back up to the end of your post?" he inquired.

"No," I replied much too quickly and loudly. I tried to regain my composure with "I think I'll just walk. It's such a pretty night."

"Suit yourself." He sounded disappointed. He slowly began to drive away. Suddenly he braked.

"Come up here, Bryant," he commanded in a dictatorial voice. With a feeling of despair, I went up to the truck.

I almost made it. Almost, I thought. *A few more seconds, and he would've been gone.* I looked in the window with a very innocent look on my face.

"Yes, Sarge?"

"The next time you challenge me, don't wait until I'm on top of you. You know better than that."

"OK, Sergeant, I sure will. Sorry about that."

As he started pulling away, he was watching me in his rear-view mirror. It seemed impossible that he had paid no attention to my pockets bulging with ammo or my missing three-and-a-half-foot-long M-16, that I was never supposed to be without. He continued watching me until he disappeared around the corner.

"Thank God, he's gone!" I sighed out loud.

"Whew!" It felt like my first breath of air in over an hour. The events of the last few minutes had sapped my energy. As I started back to the ammo shed, something shiny caught my eyes. The rounds!

Rob, you've got to start thinking. You can't afford to make any more mistakes. Satan looked at me rather curiously.

In a few minutes my relief would show up, so I had to move fast. I picked up the rounds and carefully surveyed the area for any other loose bullets that may have rolled away. Near the ammo shack I rounded the corner and grabbed my equipment can. It contained all of my dog gear which consisted of muzzle, extra choke chain, leashes, cold weather gear, and the like. I pulled off the lid and emptied my pockets. After putting a muzzle on Satan, closing the equipment can, and picking up my weapon, we headed for the end of my post.

By the time I arrived, I could see my relief coming. It was dark between the end of my post and the entry gate, but I could make out who it was. It was "Deacon Dave," our local street preacher. This guy would spout incessantly about God and Jesus and all of the heavenly hosts he and his dog had hovering around them. He wasn't offensive about it, though. If you asked him to change the subject, he would for awhile—but not for long. He normally spoke of God's love, not fire and brimstone, so he was bearable. Everyone seemed to like Deacon Dave. He was plenty of fun, always full of clean jokes.

"Hey, Rob," he called cheerfully. I gave back my greeting.

"Everything secure down there?" he asked.

"Yeah, I suppose."

"Well, praise the Lord," he responded with a smile.

By this time he was standing in front of me. I reached inside my pocket and pulled out a plastic bag containing orders which described the area borders and any special security instructions. I handed him the instructions while we both pulled our dogs close to us. Attack dogs naturally have a high opinion of their ferocity and love to prove it by killing or maiming each other. Our dogs had muzzles on, but they could still deliver nasty bites to each other. Dave put the instructions in his pocket and backed away.

"Thanks, Rob, we'll see ya." He looked down at his dog.

"Say good-bye, Major." Major barked once. As they left, Dave launched into one of his favorite hymns while Major wagged his tail.

I guess Major plans to go to heaven, too, I thought as Satan and I headed for the entry shack. My ride was waiting outside the gate to transport us back to the Command Security Control. When we reached the gate, one of the handlers, Airman Walker, started toward me as we were handing in our security badges. It was necessary to wear these badges at all times inside the nuclear storage site to confirm our clearance into the area. Baltic was still looking at me suspiciously. In order to appear calm, I struck up a conversation with Walker.

"Hey, Matt."

"Hi, Bryant," he returned, obviously not in the mood to talk.

"How was it tonight? Anything exciting happen?" I asked, trying to appear nonchalant as we walked around the shack.

"Are you kidding? Nothing exciting ever happens around here."
"Well, the reason I was asking is because my dog alerted over by the fence, kind of in your direction. Did your dog pick up anyone?" I was watching Baltic out of the corner of my eye. He was curious about Walker's answer. "Now that you mention it, he did alert once. But I didn't think anything about it at the time. Come on, let's get out of here and go home." We came to a large chain-link gate and waited a second before an electric lock clicked open. We entered and closed it behind us. We paused briefly for Baltic either to open the next gate or to search us, as was customary on a regular basis. I crossed my fingers, hoping he would not decide on a search which would include our equipment cans. In which case, I was dead. It seemed like an hour, but suddenly the next gate clicked open, and we entered. The third and final gate opened for us. I was out of the area! I let out an audible sigh of relief. Letting down the tailgate, Walker, I, and our dogs jumped into the bed of the truck. I felt as if the weight of the world had fallen from my shoulders. Somehow I had made it out of the area! *Now it's all downhill*, I thought. Man, was I in for a big surprise!

The truck driver started his route, stopping about every hundred yards or so to pick up the other relieved dog handlers and regular security troops. Three minutes and eight troops later, we arrived at CSC. We jumped out of the truck and lined up at the clearing barrel, which was used to insure that our weapons were empty. Each man inserted the muzzle of his rifle into the barrel, removed the magazine, pulled the bolt back, checked the chamber, let the bolt go, and pulled the trigger. While I waited my turn I set my equipment can down, then opened it to get out my extra M-16 magazines.

Walker was standing in front of me looking into my can. As I pulled out the last magazine a few of the .50-caliber rounds were clearly visible. I glanced up at him, but he was looking in another direction. Had he seen the rounds? After covering my can, I cleared my weapon and stood in line with the others to hand in our weapons. Walker turned in his weapon first and stepped over to our gear. He paused at mine, staring at it curiously. Nervously turning in my weapon, I grabbed my can and followed him into the truck which was now packed with the five of us and our dogs. Dogs, especially attack dogs, don't like to be crowded, so muffled growls could be heard as the truck started across the base.

We were soon across the entire base and out the main gate. The K-9 kennels were off base. This was undoubtedly decided after one of these ninety-pound killers, possibly back from Vietnam, got loose and demonstrated its attack skills on an unsuspecting GI. We pulled up at the kennels. As usual, all of us were in a hurry to put our dogs away and go home. Walker, on the other hand, seemed to be dragging his feet. After setting our gear down in front of the kennel building, we headed for the kennels themselves. Satan wagged his tail in anticipation of food and rest. I had no idea I wouldn't be taking him out the following night. Walker suddenly showed up. *What's he been doing all this time?* I asked myself. My sheer paranoia was intensifying by the second. As I headed for my car, I heard my name being called. It was Walker running over to me.

"Are you going right home?" he inquired nervously.

Walker and I didn't particularly get along, so why the sudden concern for my whereabouts?

"I don't know. Why?"

"I was just wondering. I thought I might drop over or something."

Now my paranoia had run full cycle. *What could be his motive for all of this?* I turned around and stood face to face with him. I outweighed him by at least fifty pounds, so this close confrontation made him back up a couple of steps.

"Exactly what do you want, Walker?" I asked, displaying my annoyance with playing games.

"OK, OK, but just remember I tried to be friendly about this."

"About what?" I asked.

"Never mind, you'll see."

He hurried over to his car, threw his gear in, and screeched away, his tires pelting me and my car with gravel. I shook my fist at him as he pulled out of sight.

Walker and his strange behavior naturally disturbed me. For one reason or another he was constantly trying to bother me. Maybe he was intimidated by my size—or he was working to whittle me down. I tried to dismiss him from my mind since I had other matters to consider. Namely, how I was going to go about anonymously turning the rounds in to the proper authorities? This would all be wasted if I were not successful in proving that ammunition could be stolen from a supposedly secure area. And if low-priority weapons could be stolen, maybe they would beef up security around the nuclear weapons, my most serious concern. The more I thought about it, the more excited I became. I almost laughed out loud, I was so overjoyed over what I had done.

Ten minutes later I pulled up at an apartment I shared with Tom, a fellow dog handler, and his wife, Joyce. Tom was probably my best friend. I would soon discover what a really good friend he was.

Bone tired, I went straight to my room. As I passed Tom and Joyce's room I noticed the door was slightly ajar but the light was out, so I assumed they were asleep. Quietly closing my door, I fell down on my bed, panting heavily. I whispered to myself: *The hard part's over!* For the first time since the ordeal had started I began to relax. A feeling of pride began to overtake me. *I did it,* I bragged to myself as I lay back and plotted my next move.

I had to think up a scheme to anonymously return the ammunition so the brass will know that the security breach had been carried out. They would probably suspect it was I, but just let them prove it! The ammunition wasn't inventoried, so they wouldn't know which bunker it had come from. They wouldn't even be aware on which shift it had happened, whether it was an inside job, or whether someone had managed to sneak in and out of the area. The burden of proof was on them.

Like a mischievous schoolboy, a military Huck Finn, I was beaming with "smarts" as I crawled under the sheets. *Now they'll fix the storage areas for sure.* My mind turned back to the movie "Mr. Roberts," where Ensign Pulver got away with shooting the captain with a ball of tinfoil filled with tacks. Everyone is looking for that kind of anti-hero, and yours truly was it.

Sleep slowly overtook me, and I drifted off to "Heroland." I was awakened by a loud knock on the door. My clock radio indicated I had been asleep only twenty minutes.

Who on earth could that be? I groggily staggered toward the front door, pulling on my trousers in the process. I was almost to the door when another loud knock broke the silence.

"Who is it?" I asked quietly, trying not to wake Tom and Joyce.

"Base Police, open up!"

Oh, dear Lord! my mind shrieked. My next thought was *Walker. Walker, that dirty son of a gun. I'm gonna kill him!*

There stood two Air Investigation officers. Just what I needed when it seemed my clandestine mission was accomplished! I knew one of them, Technical Sergeant Roberts. He was a tough character. Being in Security myself, I had heard about his hardball tactics.

"Yes?" I inquired, trying my hardest to look angelic.

"We need some information. Step outside please."

"Sure, how can I help you?"

"Is your name Airman First Class Robert G. Bryant?"

"Yes."

"We received an anonymous phone call to the effect that you stole some ammunition from the on-base nuclear site," he explained in a robot-like manner. What brain I had left became totally numb. After what seemed to be an hour, I blurted out, "That's ridiculous!"

"Well, in any case we want to search your person, your apartment, and your car."

Mr. Hero completely panicked.

"No, you can't. Do you have a search warrant?" I sputtered.

"No, but if you refuse I'll get one while we hold you right here. We can make life hell for you, Airman."

Suddenly I grew calm. My mind cleared. I actually had an idea!

"I tell you what. I do know something about it , but I can't talk to you here. If you'll take me back to the base, I'll tell you all about it. And I want to remain anonymous because the person I'm about to incriminate is so high up the ladder I'm afraid for my life if he finds out I talked to you."

I looked around as though I had talked too loud and perhaps someone could have heard me. The investigators looked at each other with blank expressions; my ploy seemed to confuse them.

"OK, Bryant, but this had better be good," Roberts answered, gritting his teeth.

"Oh, I think this information will blow your mind," I returned. "Let's go."

We started down the stairs when I suddenly stopped. I turned to Roberts. "Do you mind if I get my shoes and shirt?" He searched my face for a second and thought about it.

"Go ahead, but make it snappy, and leave the door open."

I went back to my room. Tom's door was still closed. Grabbing my shoes and shirt I then opened his door. He sat up. "Tom," I spoke in a stage whisper. "This is the most important thing I've ever said to you so listen. I can say this only once."

I reached into my pocket, pulled out my keys, and threw them to him.

"Come on, Bryant," a voice boomed from the hall.

"Get it out of my trunk, Tom."

"What?" he inquired.

"Let's go," Roberts hollered.

"Is that you, Rob?" came Tom's voice.

"Yeah, it's me, go back to sleep," I replied, hoping he had heard my earlier statement.

The officers escorted me out of the apartment, down the stairs, and to the back seat of their car. They slammed and locked my door. They climbed in front and pulled out.

"I thought you were trying to pull something funny back there. Now what is this important information?" Roberts prodded me.

"I'm not saying anything until we're safely behind closed doors in your office. I want it to be recorded. If I told you here, you wouldn't believe it. Also, how do I know you're not involved in this kind of thing?"

"All right, we'll play it your way, but don't think you're going to pull anything."

As we rode toward the base, there was the sound of silence. The foremost question in my mind was whether or not Tom had heard me. If he hadn't, I was in deep trouble. And even if he had, would he understand what I wanted? What if he had just shrugged his shoulders and gone back to sleep? Fifteen minutes later we pulled up in front of the investigations building. I was escorted into the small, four-room building and down a dark hall to Roberts's office. On the way we passed the jail and the law enforcement desk. I wondered if the jail would soon be occupied—by me.

Roberts unlocked the investigation room and motioned for me to sit down. He found a chair of his own and placed it in front of me. He then put one of his feet on the seat and leaned over me. Roberts motioned to the other investigator who closed the door and placed a recorder in front of my face. Roberts kept his eyes fixed on me as if he were reading my mind. He reached down and grabbed the mike.

"Investigation of alleged theft of 50-caliber rounds from the on-base nuclear site at . . ." He glanced down at his watch, then said, "1:30 AM. The next voice you hear will be that of Airman First Class Robert G. Bryant." He laid down the mike and prepared himself for a long explanation.

I paused for a second and looked squarely back at Roberts. "The reason I wanted to come back to the base and talk to Sergeant Roberts, behind closed doors, and be recorded on tape, was to make it official that I have no comment."

It required a second for my words to sink into Roberts. Slowly he looked up, his face becoming increasingly red. It seemed he would explode at any moment. He sprang forward and stormed over to me. He put his face right up to mine.

"Just what are you trying to pull, Bryant? You know you aren't going to get away with anything. You just might as well admit that you . . ." Slowly a knowing look replaced the fierce anger on his face. It was as if a brick wall had fallen on him.

"I don't believe I fell for it, Bryant. You're a sly one, but I'll getyou if it's the last thing I ever do."

He turned toward his fellow investigator. "We've been taken for a ride, Lee. Get him to the car. Now!"

Lee hauled me to my feet and pushed me out to the car. He shoved me into the backseat and locked the door. Roberts had already started the car, and we were off with a screech. He stayed at sixty miles an hour or more until we reached my apartment.

"Get out, Bryant."

I opened my door and headed for my apartment.

"Not so fast, Bryant, open your trunk."

My heart fell clear down to my toes.

"I don't have my keys," I replied rather sheepishly.

"Well, Boy, you'd better get them right now. Lee, you go with him, and don't let him out of your sight. I don't get fooled twice."

Lee knocked on the door. Tom came to the door, looking as if he had awakened from a Rip-Van-Winkle sleep. Oh, oh, I felt I was in deep trouble.

"I want Bryant's car keys," Lee said in a commanding tone.

Tom looked at me with genuine shock.

"What's going on, Rob? Who's this joker? Are you in some sort of trouble?"

"The keys," Lee repeated impatiently.

"OK, OK, where are they, Rob?"

My heart sank even deeper. Tom had no idea about what was going on.

"On my dresser," I said, trying to raise one eyebrow as a signal and hoping Tom would remember I had thrown them to him earlier.

He simply shrugged his shoulders, went back into the house, and returned a few moments later. He handed Lee the keys and cut a sidewise glance toward me.

"Really, Rob, what's going on here? I feel so helpless. What can I do."

"Nothing, Tom, you've done enough," I said kind of disgustedly.
Lee and I joined Roberts at the back of the car. "Open the trunk, Lee,"
Roberts commanded. Lee did. Even though it was dark in my trunk, the
light from my building was on the front side of the car, and I could see
that all of my gear was exactly as I had left it. Roberts grabbed my equipment can and emptied it onto the ground, revealing a muzzle, leash,
choke chain, poncho, brush, and utility belt.

The rounds were gone!

"Search the car," Roberts yelled, turning red in the face again.

I was so relieved the rounds were gone that I sat down on the curb in
an exhausted heap. Roberts and Lee proceeded literally to tear my car
apart. A sly smile crept over my face and then a chuckle until I was
laughing out loud. I couldn't control myself I was so ecstatic that Tom
had heard and understood my coded message.

To put it mildly, Roberts was now madder than a mother lion whose
cubs had been stolen. He looked at me as I was laughing and assumed I
was laughing at him. He started toward me, but Lee wedged himself between us and begged him to calm down. Then Roberts regained his composure. He looked toward the apartment and then back at me.

I shook my head from side to side as I stood up. "No search warrant,
no search," I retorted.

"Bryant, if it's the last thing I do, I'm gonna lock you up and throw
away the key. You think you've got all the bases covered, but I've already
got ideas about how to nail you," Roberts snarled.

They jumped into the car and whisked around the corner. Back in our
apartment I found Tom, with a bewildered look, just sitting. "Well, are
you gonna tell me what's going on?"

As I spilled the whole story, his eyes grew wider and wider. After I
finished, he shook his head in disbelief. "Man, I can't believe you'd do all
those things. Since you moved in here, there hasn't been a dull moment."
He paused, then continued: "What do you think Roberts will do next?"

"Oh, he'll probably get statements from everyone, then search the
storage building at the on-base site. You saw how determined Roberts is.
He isn't going to give up easily."

"Well, at least he didn't catch you in the act or with the merchandise,"
sighed. "Good night, Rob, that's enough excitement for me in one day."

"Tom, thanks."

"No problem. You would've done the same thing for me."

Overcome with curiosity, I asked, "Maybe this' just a small detail, but where did you put the ammo?"

"Ammo, what ammo?"

"Come on, the .50-caliber rounds."

"Oh, that ammo," he smirked. I put it out in the field across from the apartment complex."

He had retrieved the ammo from my trunk, had driven hastily out of the complex, and had thrown the ammo out the window. Then he said good night. *Why didn't he search my person? He could have.* The whys were mounting up. The rounds. The parts. My M-16 not with me on guard duty. My guard dog sitting outside the ammunition shed when it stood to reason I was inside that shed. Someone could have blown the whistle on me at CSC. Roberts could have searched my car before carrying me to the base. I replayed the entire scenario. It was now 2:30 AM. Four hours had elapsed since the theft—but it seemed like days.

I wonder how many people are asleep in bed without a care in the world. The smart ones. That's who!

Lying down I turned out the light. Often when in trouble, I would think back to a simpler time when I was younger and carefree. Sleep slowly overtook me. Little did I know that a fading memory from my childhood would visit me as I slept.

2
The Dream

Slowly my eyes adjusted to my dreary surroundings. I was standing on a sidewalk beside a seemingly forgotten, desolate road. The road stretched for miles in both directions and then disappeared into darkness at the horizons. How odd. The road was a one-way street.

A one-way street in a residential area was peculiar. Although the streets and sidewalks were void of people, I could hear distant voices that seemed to be coming from the sparsely placed houses lining the street. I was not particularly afraid, but I was struck with a gnawing loneliness.

Suddenly I was compelled to stroll in the direction I was facing. I had no idea why I had to go in that direction or where I was going. I merely knew I had to go. My footsteps echoed in my ears as if I were in a tunnel. After a few minutes of walking, I envisioned an end to the road—a dead end.

Where do I go from here? I asked myself. Soon I could make out an immense, Gothic-like iron gate. By the time I reached the gate, I envisioned the silhouette of an old, run-down mansion in the distance. I opened the squeaky gate. My feet carried me down a path toward the fog-enshrouded mansion. Trees and grass were all withered and dry. Flowers and brightly colored leaves were nonexistent. The house and its surroundings spoke of death and decay. No drapes were in the windows, and the shutters were hanging crookedly on their hinges. The boards were warped, and the paint was so chipped it was impossible to tell what color the house had been.

A dread foreboding swept over me. Instinctively I felt something horrible was going to transpire. For some reason I realized I had only a few minutes to escape, but I wasn't sure how.

Soon I was in the house—in a large room with no windows or doors. All I could see was a staircase at the opposite side of the room. A strong pull forced me to climb the stairs. My fear was quickly turning to panic as I drew nearer to my final destination. I ascended the stairs, fighting every step. I grabbed at the bannister and at pictures on the wall, but I could not stop my movement. At the top of the stairs the hall turned to the left. At the end of the hall, a door was barely cracked open. Again my feet dragged me in that direction. My steps echoed louder and louder in my ears. This time there was nothing to hold onto. I tried desperately to cling to the walls, but my hands slid along the slimy, cold surface. The door seemed to be calling me. In two or three more steps, I was standing in front of the door. It opened by itself, and I peered into a small room. Dark and empty, it was the most barren room I had ever seen. No furniture or pictures, only four walls and the door. I had no choice but to enter. I had the weirdest feeling I would never be able to leave that desolate place.

I took three steps and then slowly turned around. The door was no longer there! Only four walls. Frantic, I spun around and around. I was living a personal horror movie. It was a nightmare, but I didn't even know what street it was on. No door, no windows, only me and those four walls. I was entombed in a tiny, God-forsaken room at the end of an empty hall in a forgotten house at the end of an uninhabited street. And here I would stay for eternity!

"Mom! Dad!" I yelled, jumping out of my bed.

I ran across the room past my two brothers—who were awakened by the noise—and down the stairs. I opened my parents' door at a full run. It flew open and hit the doorstop with a crash. Mom rolled over and gazed at me as though she expected to see an oncoming train.

I dove for the bed, and she caught me in her arms as the bed bounced, waking up Dad. "What's going on?" he asked in a startled voice. Mom was already aware of the problem, but she asked anyhow.

"What is it, Rob?" she asked, as understanding as a person could be at three o'clock in the morning.

"Mom, I had that dream again. It's so terrible. I was all alone in that little room, and the door disappeared . . . and then I knew I'd never . . ."

"OK, it's all over now. You're fine and here with us." She held me for a minute, rocking me in her arms until I was quiet. Then she led me back up to my room. I wouldn't sleep very well the rest of the night, but at least I knew I was all right and at home. I desperately tried not to think of that awful room I felt surely I would encounter one day. I dozed off into a fitful sleep.

"Get up, Boys," came Mom's voice up the stairs.

This was the second time she had called so I decided to climb out of bed. I threw on one of my three (count 'em) Sunday suits and walked down the stairs to breakfast. I could smell the bacon and eggs. Dad was already sitting at the table reading the paper and eating. My brothers were right behind me. After saying grace, recited by a designated family member, we dove in.

My older brother Mike was *generally* quiet. Steve, my younger brother, was *always* quiet, so if I wasn't talking, which wasn't often, they noticed. Our ages were eight, seven, and three, respectively.

I guess Dad figured it was his turn to console me, since Mom had the night before. "What's wrong, Rob?" he asked with understanding eyes.

"Dad, I keep having that dream. I think it's got to mean something, 'cause it's so real—and so terrible." I paused before asking Dad the next question. I had suffered this dream about ten times, so I was desperate for an answer to its meaning or cause. *If only I could understand what was behind it, maybe it would go away.* I didn't want to appear foolish in front of my parents or brothers by asking the next question, but maybe it was the only way to find out, so I fired away.

"Dad, do you believe God could be trying to tell me something?"

I spoke the words swiftly, hoping Mike and Steve might not catch the question. It didn't work. Mike was choking on his eggs as he tried to laugh with his mouth full. Steve looked at me with wild eyes as he repeated the question several times out loud in his cute, three-year-old voice. Mom was chuckling quietly. All of us were riveted to Dad as we awaited his answer. Talk about being on the spot. He paused to reflect on my question. He sought an answer that wouldn't further embarrass me, and yet not commit himself.

"Why don't you ask Pastor Reed this morning after the service?" he asked another question. My, he looked relieved.

"Well, I hope he knows," I replied.

My heart was beating like a trip-hammer as Dad drove us to the church. Sunday School crept by like a bilious turtle. I broke out into a nervous sweat as I thought of asking Pastor Reed about my dream. Finally Sunday School and the morning service were over. I remembered nothing. When the benediction was pronounced, I ran to Pastor Reed's study. He showed up fifteen minutes later after greeting the congregation. With an inquisitive look, he asked, "Rob, were you sent here to talk to me by your Sunday School teacher?"

"Oh, no," I answered quickly.

"Well, good. What can I do for you?"

Satisfied we were alone, I spelled out the entire story, from the dream to Dad's suggestion that I talk with the pastor about it. I searched his face for a sign of emotion, but he had a deadpan expression. After I finished, he thought for a moment, crinkling his brows and staring down at his desk to formulate an opinion. I sat there anxiously awaiting his opinion of my dream. Finally he spoke.

"I'm sure, Rob, that your dream seems very real. When I was young I had similar dreams. I have to admit they can be very frightening, but it has been my experience that God speaks very rarely. When He does it is not normally to a child. However, there are cases when He might. I don't think this is one of those cases. Why would God be telling you that you are going to spend an eternity all alone in an empty room? I think the dreams will go away as you get older."

He paused. "Be sure to say hello to your parents for me. I guess you'd better go. I'm sure they're waiting for you."

The family was anxious to hear the pastor's interpretation. "Well, what did Pastor Reed have to say about your dream, Rob?" Dad inquired with genuine concern.

"He said it was a bad dream and that it'll go away someday." Everyone was satisfied with his answer . . . but me.

Several weeks later, Mike was going on his first Cub Scout camp out. He was so excited about going I felt left out. I begged Mom and Dad to let me go. They replied that seven was too young to join the Cub Scouts, but they did come up with an alternative. About an hour away was a camp for boys of all ages. I was so tickled I told Mike, "Shucks, I don't want to go to your old Cub Scout camp anyway." That next weekend Dad drove me to the camp. As we passed through the camp, my eyes almost popped out. It had everything a seven-year-old would ever want—horse stables, baseball fields, cabins, trails, a big pool, and a huge cabin-like cafeteria.

It was a young boy's paradise. During that first day, we rode horses, hiked, played all sorts of games, and ate like pigs. When night began to fall, we hit the sack, and the lights were turned out. Of course, this was followed by a half hour of monkeyshines and giggling, but soon we fell asleep from sheer exhaustion.

Oh no, my terrifying nightmare was repeating itself. I was standing in front of that door; then it opened by itself, and I was peering into that small room. Dark and empty. No furniture or pictures, only four stark walls and the door. Then I took the same three steps and then slowly turned around. The door was no longer there—only four walls. I spun around and around. No door, no windows, only me and those four walls! "Help!" I screamed at the top of my lungs.

I sat up and half jumped out of bed when I remembered where I was. Suddenly the air was filled with: "Shut up! . . . Go back to sleep, you Nut. . . . Quiet!" I tried my hardest to go back to sleep, but it was tough. For some reason I had the feeling I was very close to knowing the meaning of the dream. With this thought I finally fell asleep again.

After we stuffed ourselves at breakfast the next morning, we marched into the chapel for a religious service. We sang songs and heard a minister speak. At the end of the service he conducted what is called an invitation. He invited any of the boys who wanted to talk with a counselor about their relationship to God. He used terms like being "saved" and "born again," which were totally foreign to my church, so I kept my seat. Several of the kids responded and talked with a counselor. The rest of us were excused.

The following day the activities consisted of more baseball, horseback riding, scrumptious meals, and hiking. I was thinking of asking Dad if I could stay until I was old enough for marriage, college, or job hunting!

That night after supper we had another service, only this time it was held outdoors by a campfire. In closing, the preacher gave another invitation. He had an unusual approach, preaching that the fire represented Christ and that we should put our life into Him. If we wanted to make that commitment, he asked that we come forward and throw a stick into the fire, signifying our willingness to do so. I was among several boys who answered the invitation, but I didn't throw a stick into the fire. I just went forward and stood there. Eventually a counselor approached me.

"Why don't we sit down right over here and talk about why you came forward? OK, now, why did you come forward? I noticed you didn't throw a stick on the fire. Do you have a question about something?"

"Yes sir, I do have a question, and I ought to tell you that I've asked that question twice now. The first time I was kind of laughed at. The second time I was told that the thing worrying me wasn't bad and that it would go away."

"What would go away?" he asked with genuine concern.

Then I opened up, as fast as I could talk, about my recurring nightmare. The young man didn't appear to be shaken. He nodded all the while as though he knew what was behind the dreadful dream. He thought briefly, and then he proceeded to shock me beyond words. "I can see very clearly the meaning and the reason for your dreams." "You can?" I asked as my pulse raced.

"Yes, I feel it's as plain as the nose on your face, if you know where they're coming from and who's sending them," he explained calmly. "It's as simple as this. You're living in darkness because there is a huge thing between you and the light. The light is God. That's the reason your dream shows a dark, lonely place. Your dream is telling you about your life. I feel that the huge, old mansion is the place you're building for yourself in the next life. The Bible says we can either build a big, beautiful mansion in heaven or we can build a dark, lonely one, like the one in your dream. I think the room you enter at the end of your dream is death itself. Once there, there isn't any escape, but you can change your direction now. Your life doesn't have to end up that way.

"You see, Jesus Christ has come so we don't have to live in darkness anymore. I can't promise it, but I believe if you give your heart to Christ and accept him as your personal Lord and Savior, not only will you go to heaven, but you might not ever have that awful dream again. I'll tell you something else. God must have some great big plans for your life. God very seldom speaks to people in such an unusual way. When he does, and if we listen, we'll be blessed. If we don't, we'll be responsible. When I was young I had similar dreams. I know they can be very frightening." All of this was pretty heavy for a seven-year-old, but I did understand what he was talking about.

"Yes," I said meekly as a little tear ran down my cheek. I wasn't sure why I was crying, but somehow I recognized he was telling me the truth. I was also overcome with the thought that God could possibly be interested in me.

"Great!" he said. "I'm thrilled you're going to discover God's plan for your life. I believe He has some exciting things in store for you."

Then he led me through several Bible verses which explained how I could become a follower of Christ. I truly believed, and we closed our conversation with prayer.

The rest of camp passed uneventfully and soon I was back home.

Almost two weeks later, I dreamed I was walking down a beautiful street on a bright, sunny day. The flowers were blooming, and the birds were singing. As I skipped along, I had the odd feeling that I had been here before, but it was somehow different from what I had remembered. Then it hit me. This was the same street in my nightmare, except this time the neighborhood was illuminated. All was bright. "All things bright and beautiful . . ." I was neither scared nor nervous. No longer did I want to escape. In fact, I wouldn't have minded staying indefinitely. At the end of the street was the gate, although this time it was golden. I entered and beheld the most beautiful house I had ever seen.

I walked in, totally unafraid. There was the staircase, but it was shining from an unknown light source. Almost running, I jumped two steps at a time clear to the top. There was a door that had not existed before. It, too, glowed with brilliant colors. Reverently, I opened it. Inside was a garden filled with gorgeous plants. My eyes drank in the loveliness before me. Inside was even more breathtaking than outside. I was awe-stricken by the scene. Completely losing myself and all track of time, I explored the wonders of the garden.

Suddenly a voice broke the stillness, a friendly voice yet one that commanded respect. I felt at ease with the voice. Yet, at the same time I would have been willing to charge into battle at its summons. I don't remember the voice's exact words, but they were similar to these.

> Rob, you are My child now. If you stray from Me I will come and rescue you. Blessings will follow if you listen to Me, but tragedy will follow if you do not listen. Always remember that I love you, and I am as close as a prayer away.

Suddenly I awoke and sat up in bed. This time there was no fear—only excitement that God had spoken to me in my dream. I wondered if I were special or if God spoke to many people this way. I remained in deep thought the remainder of the night. The following morning, it seemed I was walking on a cloud. My parents noticed a marked change in my behavior and asked what was wrong. My first reaction was not to tell them about my new dream, but I was bubbling with excitement. The dam of my pent-up emotions burst. I told the family all about summer camp and about my new dream. This time they really appeared to be happy for me. Years later I discovered that one of my parents had told my story to some relatives and they had laughed. I was heartbroken.

The years passed, and the dream faded into a vague memory. As far too many of them do, my parents divorced. Also, as many do, I stopped going to church during my high-school years. I am happy to report that my Mom and Dad both eventually remarried.

In 1973, at age eighteen, I joined the U.S. Air Force.

3
"You're Going to Jail, Boy!"

After four hours of sleep, I wearily opened my bloodshot eyes. I felt as if I had swallowed a dirty, but dry, dishrag.

My first thoughts were of the dream that repeated itself the night before. I hadn't thought about that series of dreams in the last thirteen years. Why had they risen from the grave of my memory? It seems I was reliving my childhood in a dream. *Was there any substance to its recurrence? Was I being contacted again? God had promised that if I wandered, He would come and rescue me,* I thought. Finally I shrugged my shoulders, trying to dismiss these thoughts and concentrating on my plan of action. Roberts had not been exaggerating. I was in deep trouble.

As I dressed, I talked with myself. *Keep a cool head. Steady, Boy.* I sounded like I was talking to my dog Satan. *Good grief, what a name!* I tried to shake the cobwebs loose so I could face a distressing day with at least a half-clear mind. I began thinking of how I would investigate the case if I were Roberts. Then, perhaps I could guess his moves one step ahead of him. *My first move would be to investigate the scene of the crime. I would take fingerprints from the building and equipment. I don't believe I touched any smooth surfaces. OK twice. Then I would look around the area. I'm OK there too. Nothing but military bootprints would be around the area, and they couldn't distinguish mine from anybody else's.*

I ran into my room and looked at the soles of my boots. On my right boot sole was a gash running almost two inches long! My heart sank even lower. These bootprints would be unique and easily traced to the scene.

Hey, pull yourself back together. Maybe they won't check footprints. "Oh yeah, fat chance!" I hollered out loud.

They'll have Sergeant Baltic's testimony that I wasn't on my post when he drove by. Perhaps that'll be offset by Walker's statement that his dog had alerted on someone during the night. A strong case could be built around an outside force's copping the ammo. But of course the most dam-

27

aging testimony will be from Walker if and when he says he saw the ammo in my equipment can. *They have the testimony of the supervisors about my boasting that anyone could steal from the nuclear storage areas—and that one day I would prove it. Boy, was that stupid!*

But thanks to Tom the evidence wasn't found where they thought it would be. Of course, Roberts figured out too late why I insisted he bring me back to the base for interrogation. Now the big question was, *"Could he prove it?"*

It's a marvel I didn't slash my throat shaving because I uttered the statement that would be shouted at me for the next several weeks:

"You're going to jail, Boy!"

I immediately checked with Tom as to the whereabouts of the ammunition he had thrown into the field. I carefully looked over my shoulder and all around for any would-be followers. It looked clear. I drove to the field and parked behind a nearby tree. I ran to the area where Tom had thrown the rounds. Sure enough, there they were stacked in three or four piles not more than thirty feet from the road. I looked around one more time to make sure I was alone. With the rounds in my pockets, I drove away to implement the next phase of my plan.

Ten minutes later, I arrived at the base's front gate. My plan was simple: take the ammo to an area that was publicly accessible yet near the on-base site and dump it there. The spot I chose was between the lake and a park. Soon after I dropped it, the ammo would be found, and it wouldn't be traceable to any one person—and the burden of proof would rest on Roberts.

Four or five vehicles were between my car and the front gate. Each of the three gates was guarded by an Air Force law enforcement officer. Only those cars with a base sticker on their bumper or individual permission to enter were allowed inside. A guard would glance at each bumper one by one and wave the vehicles through. Finally he came to me, looked down at my bumper, and waved me through. Seeing no more cars behind me, he glanced back. We exchanged mutual nods as I pulled away. First he peered down the road for any oncoming traffic. Suddenly he turned around and stared at my license plate—then started waving his arms frantically at me. I continued driving as if I hadn't seen him. As I rounded the next corner I could see in my mirror that he was radioing me into Command Security Control (CSC).

Soon law enforcement cars would surround me, and investigators would surely find the bullets in my car. Now I didn't have time to dispose of the ammo at the arranged place. The base speed limit was twenty-five miles per hour. It was killing me, but I kept driving the speed limit so I might not be stopped. I turned left at the commissary, and drove though a parking lot packed with vehicles. Uh, oh! I saw a law enforcement car, headed for the front gate, pass the spot where I had just been on the road. I stopped and waited for the other car to disappear. When the coast was clear, I pulled onto a road that led toward another gate. I had to get out of there fast. I aimed my car toward the back gate and prayed.

In thirty seconds, I was approaching the gate. The guard was talking with a driver who was trying to gain access. I pulled through the gate slowly. As usual the guard paid little attention to departing traffic since he was busy with the entering. But I thought this was strange because he should have been alerted by that last radio transmission. Nevertheless, I was through, so I began thinking of my next move.

This particular road passed the kennels. I didn't know what to do or where to go, so I drove into the kennel parking lot. My pursuers would assume I was still inside the base and would start a peripheral search from the point where I had been spotted. They could have alerted the civilian police, so I didn't want to travel too far off base with the ammo. So, here I was, right back where I started with the ammo. This was definitely not part of my plan. Obviously it was time to improvise.

Sergeant Baker came striding out the front door of the kennel administration building. He was the most easy-going Sergeant we had and I counted him as a close friend. I needed all the help I could get, and maybe Baker was my last hope. I grabbed all the ammo off the seat and threw my door open.

"Sergeant Baker," I cried helplessly. "Wait, I need to talk with you right away."

"Sure, Bryant, just let me go out into the kennels and . . ." He spied the ammo in my hands as I ran toward him. His usually ruddy face bleached out.

"What in the world are you doing with those rounds?"

"There's no time to explain. Please, Sergeant, you've got to help me!"

"So it's true. You did steal the rounds. Sergeant Roberts alerted the kennel master about it, but up until now, I didn't believe it. This morning everybody and his brother was out at the on-base site. They went through the small arms building with a fine-tooth comb."

"Are you alone?" I asked hurriedly.

"Yes."

"OK, let's go inside, and I'll tell you all about it."

As we walked into his office, we looked all around to make sure we were not spotted. Baker was taking a calculated risk by not immediately blowing the whistle on me. We sat close to a window where we could watch for any unwanted guests. I spilled my guts to him. Easy-going as he was, he nearly fell apart as I finished. For what seemed like a long time, he sat there staring at me with wild eyes. During those agonizing moments, I couldn't tell if he was for or against me.

"OK. I can see only one way out of this predicament. We'll have to trust each other, and I'll have to trust you—and hope you're not going to break under questioning. Roberts can be tough and very tricky . . . and you'll have to trust me not to turn you in. We're in this together now. Agreed?"

"Yes Sir, you know you can count on me. What do you want me to do?"

Paranoid as I was, I had slight reservations, but I never really dreamed he was willing to help. Besides, what choice did I have?

"Of course," Sergeant Baker thought out loud, "the easy way out is just to hide or destroy the evidence. But if you're determined to turn in the ammo to prove a point, I see only one way to do it. It's dangerous, and probably the trickiest. They still think you're on the base, right?" he asked, scratching his chin as he thought.

"Right."

"Well, then, here's what you do. Leave the ammo here with me. Then you go to the far end of the base and enter again by the hospital gate. Then drive straight to the investigation office and say you want to talk to Roberts. In the meantime, I'll call Roberts and say I found some ammo. You see, if you go to his office and supposedly you haven't left the base, they can't link the evidence to you. Besides, you never left Walker's sight last night while you were here. According to his testimony the ammo was in your possession when you left the kennels." He paused. "I have no idea if he'll buy all of this, but it's the best I can come up with in such a short time. Do you have any other suggestions?"

"No, I'm too tired and scared to think."

"Well, you'd better start thinking when you talk to Roberts. I told you he's cunning. Now go and good luck."

I took off toward the other side of the base. Ten minutes later, I pulled up to the gate. The guard was checking IDs of the personnel departing. I knew law enforcement was looking for me to leave the base, not reenter. Maybe he wouldn't notice me. He glanced over his shoulder and saw my car, waved me through, and turned back to the line of leaving cars. I drove in and slowly pulled away from the gate. As I watched him in my mirror, he continued to check leaving vehicles. I pulled safely around a corner out of his sight.

"Whew," I sighed out loud, wiping my brow.

So far, so good. So good? Who are you trying to kid? What if Sergeant Baker turns you in? Even if he doesn't, Roberts will never believe any of this. If he's got any brains at all, he'll figure out this masquerade.

I drove straight to Investigations and was promptly met by Roberts, who was wearing an almost fatherly smile. "I knew I'd see you bright and early this morning. I thought you'd come around. Let's talk and have a cup of coffee together. I'm on your side. I want you to believe that. If you'll confide in me, I'll see that the military goes easy on you."

He led me to his office where we both sat down. He pulled out his familiar recorder and a pad of paper. "OK, Rob, go ahead. How did you do it, and where are the rounds of ammunition? I promise I'll go easy on you if you tell me how you did it. All we want to do is find out what happened. Who knows, you might get a commendation for finding a security problem."

He turned on the recorder and called out for his assistant who came in and closed the door behind him. Somehow I felt Roberts was lying through his teeth. If he had really meant what he said, he would have said it in front of his witness and would have recorded it. I cleared my throat and squirmed in my seat.

"I didn't come to confess. I came to talk about last night. I couldn't sleep because of the accusations you made against me. What makes you think I did it? Can you prove anything is missing? Besides, Walker has had it in for me a long time. You can ask any of the other guys. He's probably making up this story in order to incriminate me of something while pulling a little stunt of his own. Anyway, you searched me and my car last night. Why don't you search my apartment? I don't have anything to hide. If I had anything to hide would I have come . . .?"

Then the phone jangled. "Hello. Yes, this is Sergeant Roberts. You did? Where? When? Did you see anybody? OK, I'll be right there. He hung up and had a sadistic snarl on his face. "We've got you now, Bryant. I don't know who you think you're playing with, but I'm going to see to it that you no longer wear this uniform. You are going to regret the day you decided to join this outfit.

"Because you're going to jail, Boy. Not just any old jail, but military prison. Take a good look at this face because this is the face that is going to put you there. By the way, you are relieved of duty as of right now. Turn in your badge to Sergeant Vincent, the kennel master. You will work permanent CQ until further notice. Now get out of here!"

He and his partner stormed out of the room. His words rang in my ears ... "Because you're going to jail, Boy. Not just any old jail, but military prison." I kept thinking that this was all a bad dream. *I mean, come on, this' good old Rob we're talking about. I'm not a bad person. I just wanted to prove a point. I really didn't do anything that bad, did I?*

Being permanent CQ meant I would be staying behind each night at the kennels while my fellow squad members would be patroling their posts. CQ was considered a choice assignment, often given as a reward for good work. So this meant my squad was going to be denied the privilege of CQ. They were not going to like this. I hoped they wouldn't hate me so much they would turn on me and help Walker and Roberts put me away.

When I reached home, I told Tom and Joyce about my morning. As always, they tried to cheer me up. I apologized to Tom for involving him. I arrived back at the kennels at one o'clock in the afternoon. The Kennel Master, Sergeant Vincent, and Sergeant Baker were there. Vincent motioned for me to come into his office. Shaking his head at me for a few seconds, he began to speak in a quiet voice. I was amazed that he was not angry—he was sad, not mad. "Rob, I can't believe you'd take such a big risk just to prove a point. I mean, eventually they would've done something about the lack of security. Now they're gonna nail you to the wall. Why didn't you write a letter about the poor security measures? Was your escapade worth it?"

"Sarge, I'd rather not talk about it. Besides, how can you be sure that I did anything?"

"Well, it's not me you have to worry about. Roberts is sure, and he's out to nail you. You embarrassed him badly last night when you pulled that little trick of bringing him back to the base. He's really angry, angrier than I've ever seen him. According to Roberts, he's got more proof than he'll need to send you to prison. The fact is, we could all lose our stripes over this incident. So now it's not just Roberts who's involved. The word is out that you've brought the attention of the big brass. They'll probably make an example out of you, then lock you up before anybody hears about it. I'm sorry, Rob, but I'll have to take your security badge and shield."

Eyes are everywhere, I reminded myself. Baker was standing over by the door nervously looking around. He refused to look at me. When I tried to make him speak, he shook his head. "Not here—outside," he whispered.

Out behind the kennels, we whispered with the jitters. Baker confided, "I told Roberts I had found the ammo, just like we planned. But he didn't believe me; he even led me down to his office to question me. He's sure you did it and wants me to testify against you. I told him I didn't know anything about it—I just found the ammo. I doubt if he believed me, but I'll have to stick to my story, or I'll be breaking rocks right along-side you. Just remember, we're in this together, and they still have to prove you're guilty. Just don't get nervous, and you'll make it."

"OK, I'll keep cool. He won't get anything out of me. Thanks for help-ing out."

"Forget it. Let's pretend it never happened," he said, trying to sound cool. I gave my canine companion, Satan, a workout for the rest of the afternoon (this would become a daily routine in the weeks to come). Fi-nally, the rest of the squad started to arrive, and we fell in for an informal guard mount. This meant that Vincent would inspect our uniforms and grooming and fill us in on pertinent news for the day. The last item on his agenda was filling us in about my being assigned to permanent CQ. There were a few moans and groans, and then we were dismissed. As we fell out, Walker made a beeline for Sergeant Vincent's office.

"Sergeant Vincent, may I have a word with you?" Walker inquired, looking back at me with a twisted grin on his face.

They walked into Vincent's office and shut the door. After my fellow guards encouraged me, we went into the building to play cards until it was time for our posts. I was curious about how they had discovered my predicament. (I was later informed that the news was all over the base that a culprit had stolen something important from the on-base nuclear site). After a half hour, Walker, grinning smugly, emerged from Vin-cent's office. Vincent was concerned about me, yet he had the responsi-bility of enforcing regulations. He would help Roberts and Walker only if he had to, but luckily for me he didn't know anything about my stunt.

Vincent and Baker left at five o'clock. The guys and I played spades and shot the bull until about eight PM. Walker sat and watched TV in a corner of the room. After one of the hands of spades, two of the men left to work out their dogs. This left three of us and Walker. One of the members of the squad winked at me and whispered to one of the other men, "Now, it's time for fun and games."

"Hey, Walker, come on over and play a few hands—we need a fourth."

"No thanks," Walker replied snappily.

"Come on, we're not going to bite."

"No, I don't think so, I'm watching a good movie," he came back nervously.

The other men kept razzing him until he turned off the TV and joined us. Campbell, on my immediate right, suddenly jumped up and moved across the table from me. This left the open chair beside me. Walker hesitated, then sat down slowly, glancing at me out of the corner of his eye. I just stared at him. With his concentration on me, and not on the game, Walker made one stupid play after another. I made the situation worse by continuing to stare at him while the other guys snickered.

Soon it was time for the squad to leave. We played one last hand. On the last trick, I grabbed Walker's arm with a strong grip. His little arm was like a small branch in my hand. He tried not to become jumpy, but how do you remain calm while your arm is being fractured? Finally he spoke with a pained voice. "Get your hands off me unless you want to add assault to your charges."

The rest of the squad looked on with interest.

"Walker, if you don't go to Investigations tomorrow morning and tell them you made up the whole story, or that you're not sure of what you saw, I'll kill you."

I couldn't believe the words that had burst from my mouth. What really scared me was not knowing whether or not I meant it. Was I losing control of myself? I let go of his arm. He rubbed the red area on his forearm as we gazed at each other.

"Now you're in big trouble, Bryant. I've got witnesses to this."

He looked around at the other guys. They either looked down or away.

"You heard him, didn't you?" Walker urgently asked.

"Heard what?" one of the guys commented, and they laughed as they walked out the door.

Walker, realizing he was alone with me, ran out the door. I stepped outside and perched on a bench outside the door. The men and their dogs soon boarded the truck. Then came Walker with his dog and gave me a dirty look as if to say, "I dare you to try something." It appeared he was ready to turn his dog loose on me if I came too close. The truck pulled away.

The following afternoon at three o'clock, I was back at the kennels for another day of CQ. Sergeant Vincent gave me word that I was expected to meet with Roberts in Investigations.

I supposed he wanted to talk to me about Walker's sudden change of story. Walker couldn't prove I had threatened him, so I momentarily felt fairly good about matters. When I reached his office, he started with the same routine. He turned on his tape recorder and called a witness.

"Sit down, Bryant," he said with a seemingly friendly voice. I wondered if he were simply playing another one of his character parts.

"Bryant, I thought we had a pretty good case against you from the beginning. But something happened this morning to change my mind. You see, Walker just left here. Yes, he told me something that changes your case drastically. It seems that yesterday at 7:45 PM at the kennels you verbally threatened Airman Walker's life in front of three witnesses. Now we don't have a good case—we have an excellent one! Not only does this add assault to the list, but it is really an admission of guilt.

"So with this new evidence your company commander has given me permission to proceed with charges that will be reviewed at your very own court martial. I just wanted you to be aware of these new and exciting developments. You'll work the 8 AM-to-5 PM shift at the kennels until further notice. You can go now . . . and, hey Bryant, have a nice day. Oh, and by the way, if I were you, I'd get a good lawyer. You're gonna need all the help you can get. Who knows? Maybe he can get you off with ten years of hard labor. Now, get out of here before I get sick to my stomach at the sight of you."

When I reached the apartment I confided in Tom and Joyce. "Cheer up," Tom tried to lighten the situation. "Things couldn't get any worse," he quipped. I soon discovered he was wrong.

The following morning, I reported to the kennels and began work right away. I figured the harder I worked, the less I would think about my new home in prison. As I cleaned the place, I became serious about finding an attorney. During lunch I stopped by the legal building to talk with one.

A few minutes later, I was sitting in an empty waiting room, wondering how many other military personnel were in trouble. I imagined others might have left the base and hired a civilian lawyer. Symbolically, I shook my pockets. They were empty, as usual.

Well, I guess this is the only one in town I can afford, I mused. Not long after, a military attorney stopped at the desk where I was signed in. "Airman Bryant, you're next," he called out, extending his hand for a shake. "OK, Airman Bryant, go ahead. Don't leave anything out, even if it seems unimportant to you. I want you to be totally honest. Anything you say in the confines of this room, I am bound to keep a secret. Anything you say will remain strictly confidential. I am on your side, so let's work as a team from the very beginning. The only way I can help you is if you trust me with the whole story. Go ahead and feel free to start talking, and I'll listen. I'll take notes and ask questions when necessary."

"The whole thing started about six months ago when I informed my superiors about the lack of security. They laughed at me and said I was crazy. Then, I started planning a theft. I thought I had a foolproof plan, but as it turned out a few unexpected circumstances threw my plan off course. You see, on the night I actually pulled it off . . ."

Like a dam that had burst I poured out the entire escapade. I talked nonstop for at least half an hour. As I talked, a look of disbelief began showing on his face. He took notes as fast as he could go. I could also tell by his expression and all the bold print on his pad that he thought I was in deep trouble. After I finished, he sat for a moment reviewing his notes that now filled over three pages. As he raised his eyes toward mine, there was a look of pity on his face.

"Let me get this straight. During the actual theft you were discovered to be off your post by the area sergeant. Then the ammo was seen in your possession by Airman Walker as you left CSC. Then later you led Investigative Sergeant Roberts away from the ammo and involved Airman Brooks in your crime. On the following morning you drove to the base with the ammo on your seat, almost getting stopped by base police entering and leaving the base. And then on the advice of one Sergeant Baker you left the ammo at the kennels, not only narrowing the theft to a K-9 handler but also incriminating Sergeant Baker. He then proceeded to lie to Sergeant Roberts about having found the ammo by accident. And then in the presence of three witnesses, you threatened the life of Airman Walker. Not only did this add to your charges, but it is a witnessed admission of guilt.

"Furthermore, if they can link you with some subversive organization, they're going to say you stole it in order to sell it or, even worse, to give that organization help in sabotaging our government. They will probably assume you have been doing this for some time. And to top it all off, you told several of your supervisors months ago that you were going to do it.

I don't suppose you thought to wear gloves while you were in the building either."

I nodded my head in a no. He shook his head and stared at me with a perplexed, but stern, look.

"What is it you want me to do for you? You already have people who are going to have to perjure themselves to save you. Do you want me to lie for you too? If I were the prosecution, I would let anyone of them off scot-free for telling the truth about their part in the incident.

"Believe me, you have only one recourse. That is to turn yourself in and bargain for a lesser charge. If you plead innocent, you'll have to perjure yourself in a court of law. They'll nail you up to dry. Just on these charges alone you could get seven years hard labor at Leavenworth. Don't you see they're going to have to make an example out of you? If not, we'll have everyone breaking the law in order to prove something."

He paused again. "That's my advice—turn yourself in. I can probably get you off with four, maybe three years of hard labor."

"No," I returned defiantly. "I want you to get me off. Isn't there any way you can?"

"Are you kidding? It's only a matter of time before they put it all together. If I were Roberts, I would hound all of the witnesses until they talked. That is, if they haven't already talked. So let's be sensible about this."

"If being sensible means going to jail, I'm not playing your way."

"OK, but don't forget, I tried to warn you. At this point the best I can do is talk to Investigations and see what they can tell me. I'll also look up some regulations and military law that I'm not really up on. Until you hear from me, don't answer any more questions, unless I'm present."

"Thanks for your help. I hope to hear some good news from you soon." I felt as if I were whistling in a dark cemetery.

As I left in a daze, I kept asking myself, *What on earth are you going to do? What are you going to do?*

That night I decided it was about time to call my dad. When I was young, most of the time he seemed to have an answer. Maybe he could help now. Even if he couldn't, I desperately needed to hear his voice. I not only could use some advice, but he would probably rather hear the story from me than read it in some newspaper. I called him in New York where he was living at the time.

"How are you, Dad?"

"Rob?"

"Yeah, it's me, Dad."

"What's going on, Son?"

That's a loaded question, I thought to myself. I had no idea where to start. I wasn't even sure I wanted to tell him the truth. In fact, I had been having difficulty handling the truth for a long while. I decided to lay my cards on the table. "Dad, I'm in a lot of trouble. I've done a really dumb thing. At the time it seemed like the thing to do. Now I'm not sure. It all sounds worse than it really is. You see, I stole this ammo to prove it could be done. Then one thing led to another, and now I've got several other charges against me. I think I might go to jail. I just don't know what to do. I need some advice. What do you think I should do?"

There was a long silence on the other end of the line. Finally came these words that I shall never forget.

"Rob, of my three boys, you were always the most extreme. When you ran, you were the fastest. When something needed doing, you did it. Whatever you attempted, you gave it your best shot. You were outgoing, decisive, and a born leader. Having those qualities are good, if kept under control. Control is something that comes with age and learning. When you were young, you weren't controlled. If you remember, you were also in the most trouble and in the most fights . . . and you spoke most often before thinking. I had hoped that by now you would have developed the good side of your attributes, but it seems you chose to use the negative. I'm not surprised you're in trouble, but I am very sad. There's nothing I can do for you other than to pray. Son, I hope God will give you the wisdom to know what to do."

When he finished, I mumbled that I would try to work it out and would consider his counsel. But now I felt totally dead inside. After asking how the family was, I hung up. Two hours later my relief arrived.

Fitfully trying to sleep that night, I heard my father's disappointed voice as though it were a requiem. Yes, smart-aleck Rob had messed up. I had driven another nail in my father's coffin. And his references to God were strange. Other than going to church on Sundays, he had never mentioned God. The pain struck me straight in the heart.

He was absolutely right about my character. I was too big for my britches, to use an expression of an earlier era, and I had continued to follow the negative side of my personality instead of the good. I also started hearing other voices during the night . . .

the words of Deacon Dave
the military attorney
Sergeant Roberts
Walker
Sergeant Vincent.
"God loves you."
"We are investigating a theft on the on-base site."
"You are relieved of duty."
"I'm so disappointed in you."
"You're going to jail, Boy!"
"Give me your badge and shield."
"Confess."
"Plead guilty."
"Seven years of hard labor."
"I'll pray for you."
"God will give you wisdom."

I also thought about the bad dream that had resurfaced only days before, and the words of the counselor at the camp. "God must have some awfully big plans for your life. Not often does God speak to people. When he does, and if we listen, we will be blessed. If we don't, we will be held accountable."

Then I heard the voice from the dream after my prayer at camp. "Rob, you are My child now. If you stray from Me, I will come and get you. Blessings will follow you if you listen to My voice. Always remember that I love you and I am as close as a prayer away."

Could all the events of the past few weeks have come about as God's plan to draw me back to Himself? I could not help but wonder. Maybe He allowed all of this in order to make me recognize I needed Him, especially since the dreams of my youth had resurfaced.

I rolled off the bed and onto my knees. I had hardly prayed in years, so I wasn't sure what to say or where to start. All I understood was: This prayer became to me the most important thing in the world. I folded my hands just like I did as a kid. It didn't seem childish at all. I looked up toward the ceiling and prayed, "Oh God, I don't know exactly what to say to You, but I'm sorry for the way I've acted. I'm scared about what is happening around me and even more, I'm scared about the person I am becoming. God, please forgive me. When I gave my heart and life to You in summer camp thirteen years ago, I told You that I was Yours and that I would listen to You. Well, I haven't and I'm sorry about that too. I know You said You would never leave me and I know that You haven't. I believe that I need You more now than I ever have before. Thank You for allowing this to happen because I know that I will be close to You again. I know what You are thinking. You think that I'm just saying this because I am in trouble. Maybe that is true, but I promise for the rest of my life I will serve You, even if I have to go to prison for what I have done. Let me know if I can do anything for You. Give me a try. Amen."

During my prayer, I didn't see angels or see visions. But I was sure that I had just talked to the Creator of the universe, and that if anybody could help, He could. After my prayer, all of the haunting voices were gone. I was going to let tomorrow take care of itself. I quit worrying. Tonight I was going to sleep well for the first time in several days. I slowly drifted off to sleep.

4
A New Beginning

Boring . . . but also nerve wracking . . . cleaning the kennels during the day and hanging around my apartment at night . . . talking with my attorney a few more times . . . being badgered to confess by Investigations . . . I thought if I heard the words, "You're going to jail" or "Turn yourself in" or "Make it easy on yourself; confess and we'll go easy on you" one more time, I would scream.

All I could do was hope, trust, and pray. Somehow after my prayers, I felt I could handle it; whatever happened, I was no longer alone. There was no doubt in my mind that God had allowed me to bottom out so I could return to fellowship with Him.

One morning I was informed that the flight officer wanted to meet with me at once. I dropped what I was doing and drove to CSC. There, the company commander, the flight officer, and the flight sergeant were waiting.

"Airman Bryant reporting as ordered, Sir," I addressed the flight officer, a colonel. A full colonel is five steps down from God to an airman first class. He finally acknowledged my presence with a casual salute. "Airman Bryant, a command just came down from SAC (Strategic Air Command) Headquarters concerning you."

SAC Headquarters! I thought to myself. *I had no idea SAC was in on this. Good grief! I am in woefully deep trouble!*

"I think what you've done is disgusting. It reeks of misconduct, disregard for authority, and downright treason. We're trying to countermand this order because it's not the one we're seeking." He reached into his top desk drawer and pulled out my badge and shield and handed them to me. I could hardly believe this turn of events. It was nothing short of miraculous.

"However, until further notice, you are hereby returned to active duty. Report to the kennels tomorrow for duty assignment. That was for the record. Now let me tell you something off the record. We are going to be watching you, Bryant. If you spit on the sidewalk, we'll rake you over the coals. Now get out of my sight."

Trying to contain my exhilaration, I calmly closed the door—then let out the loudest "Yahoo" ever recorded. I leapt like a dancing Watusi, sped like a gazelle, and yelled like a banshee. Sprinting past my car, I crossed the base, yelling, "I'm free, I'm free!" When I stopped running, I found myself at the kennels.

For the first time in over a month I laughed and kidded around. I invited all of the personnel to a "Freedom Party" I planned to host the following weekend at my apartment. I immediately called my parents and other friends to share the news that the investigation was over and that I was free.

That night I once again thanked Tom and Joyce for their encouragement and support through my ordeal. I also made arrangements to move out of their apartment and into my own. I would remain friends with them for a long time. *Now, with my own apartment,* I thought, *I'm gonna live.*

The following morning, I dressed in full uniform as though I had been invited to serve as the President's personal honor guard. I headed for Investigations. I had several questions about my release—like why, who ordered it, and how? I asked for Roberts who was not in. His assistant turned crimson in the face.

"If you know what's good for you, you'll get out of here," the assistant snarled. "If Roberts sees you he might just decide to sacrifice one of his stripes for the pleasure of beating the daylights out of you. But before you go, just tell me one thing. Who do you know in high places? Who would care enough to stick their neck out to release you? Not that it matters. We're busy trying to find out who. When we do, we'll reverse their decision, and you'll be prison bound where you belong. This little stunt of yours isn't going to work."

As I left I wondered what on earth he was talking about. Why didn't Investigations know the origin of the order? Next, I consulted my attorney, thinking maybe he had been instrumental in my release. He knew even less than Investigations. For several months curiosity almost killed this cat. I heard all kinds of weird rumors which I am not privileged to repeat, but I could pin down none of them.

No cohesive answer was forthcoming; it seems I will never know for sure, but my lawyer did explain to me that the conditions for my release were such that Investigations needed far more evidence to put me away. All existing charges had been dropped, so Investigations would need something new or overlooked in order to resurrect charges against me. My counsel also thought it would be difficult for them to dig up additional evidence since Investigations already had such a good case against me. I figured, though, that Roberts wouldn't let it rest. Since his reputation was riding on this, he probably would carry on his own investigation, even though the Air Force had closed the case. My counsel advised me to shut up about it—simply do my job and stay away from trouble. But as I would find out later, trouble was hard for me to avoid.

The day after my release I drove to the kennels at the usual time. All of the other dog handlers started arriving, but Walker never showed up. However a replacement K-9 trooper was in his place. It was Dave Koksma, better known as "Deacon Dave." Satan and I had a happy reunion. As the others entered the building I stayed outside with my canine sidekick. Ah, it was fantastic for both of us to be free!

As I was putting Satan back into his kennel, Sergeant Vincent called to me: "Rob, we need to talk for a moment."

"Sure, Sarge. Boy, it feels good to be back on the squad."

"I'm glad you're back, too, and that's what I wanted to talk with you about. As I'm sure you noticed, Walker didn't show up today. I moved him to another squad. He decided that working with you would be dangerous for him. I think he's right. Rob, I don't want any trouble out of you concerning Walker. He's agreed to stay away from you. I want the same agreement from you."

"No problem, Sarge. I don't want any trouble either. I'm free, and I want to stay that way. I think you're wise, though, to move him. I'm afraid if I had to look at his face everyday, I'd be tempted to rearrange it."

"OK, just keep your temper under control, and I'll keep Walker away from you. Remember that Roberts will be watching your every move."

"It's a deal." We walked back into the building together talking about the new squad arrangements. Soon after, he dismissed us for dinner. At mess I answered the squad's questions about the investigation and why I had been released. But I carefully guarded my words. Most of my answers were yes-and-no types.

We were back on our respective posts within an hour. Ironically enough I was assigned to the on-base site, and who do you suppose was the Area Sergeant? Baltic! Was it a fluke or was there a design to this assignment? I soon found out. I walked back and forth on my post. I didn't take one step off the road. I wouldn't even look at the small arms building. Slowly the hours passed, and then I had only an hour left. After completing one of my rounds, Satan suddenly alerted on someone. There was no mistake. Someone was approaching from the entry point. At that instant I had no idea how far away they were—only that they were close enough for my dog to smell them. Though he could smell a person as far away as several hundred yards, I certainly couldn't judge the distance.

"Where is he, Boy?"

He pointed his nose upwind and continued to sniff, tugging hard in the direction the person or persons were approaching. Satan was quieter than the proverbial mouse, following his training perfectly. Because of this special training and rapport of guard and dog, I knew where the intruder was, but he didn't know where we were. We slowly moved up one side of the bunkers. Satan was becoming more excited. The intruder was awfully close now. Crouching on the top, we could see someone coming toward us.

Baltic. We were still undetected when he walked right past us. We waited as he tiptoed slowly beyond the bunker. He was about twenty feet from us as we crept down off the bunker behind him. We stole up behind him for several yards. Satan was enjoying this tracking game and did not growl. After several steps, we passed a light, and my shadow moved forward in front of him. Without warning, he twirled around quickly, grabbing his M-16 off his shoulder as he pivoted. Even before the turn was complete, his left hand was under the gun barrel and his right hand was on the trigger housing. In an instant the weapon was pointed toward my abdomen. This was definitely a move he had learned in Vietnam.

"Now that I have your attention, and if you're through playing games, I have a message for you," Baltic spoke with a chill in his voice.

Satan was out at the end of his leash, growling, and he knew Baltic's greeting was anything but friendly. I called Satan off, and he grudgingly returned to the heel position, never once removing his eyes from Baltic. Baltic had caught me off guard. I wasn't sure if he had seen my shadow at the last second or if he really had known where I was the whole time. I tried not to act shocked by his actions.

Speaking through clenched teeth, he lit into me verbally: "Because of your stupid, irresponsible actions a month ago, several of us have marks against our records. You might even have made some of us ineligible for re-enlistment. If that happens I wouldn't give a 'plug nickel' for your life.

They'll find you in a ditch somewhere or run over by a car. But in the meantime, my friends and I will be watching you, and somehow we'll get you. I don't know what you pulled, or who you know, to get put back on duty. But it won't last long if I have anything to do with it. Just remember wherever you go in this man's Air Force, someone will be watching you. And one more thing, next time challenge me as I walk by, or I'll have those stripes. Now get back to work and keep your eyes open."

He disappeared back into the darkness from which he had come. Satan watched Baltic until he was satisfied he was gone. I made a decision after this encounter that I was going to play the game according to the book until the day of my discharge.

In the days that ensued I continued to operate according to the rules, but strange changes began happening in and to me. Soon I actually wanted to obey the rules and be a good example. Whatever was transpiring— even though I didn't understand it—I liked it. It dawned on me that I should have operated like this the whole time, but my flair for testing parameters had almost destroyed my life.

Soon it was Saturday, the day of the freedom party at my apartment. Bill, my new roommate, and I prepared for the party. We bought enough liquor for a small army and all kinds of party snacks. By seven o'clock members of all three squads started arriving. We expected about thirty people which included some Security Police troops. By 7:30, almost all of them had arrived and were heading toward a drunken stupor. I had invited Deacon Dave, but he declined. I rightly figured his religious beliefs were inhibiting him. I was too busy to drink since I was opening the door and serving drinks and food nonstop.

At around nine o'clock, I finally sat down with a beer. I looked around the room. These guys and girls were crocked. Suddenly I realized that no one had even congratulated me at my own freedom party! As a matter of fact, they were sitting around becoming drunk on my booze, and no one even cared enough to talk with me. For the first time, as if a light had come on, I realized how self-centered all my friends were. They probably wouldn't have cared if this had been a freedom party or a jail party. It was merely a reason to get together and get drunk. I downed my beer, hoping it would change my thoughts. It didn't work.

I tried to be involved with the party, but the jokes were so filthy and the language so blasphemous I couldn't get with it. I was embarrassed in my own apartment. I seemed totally out of place. Even the beer tasted different, and I didn't want the liquor for some reason. I tried to smile and laugh, but it all seemed empty and meaningless. I was a little mad at myself for not having a good time. I suffered through it somehow and by three AM almost everyone was gone. Bill saw the last few to the door, and I hit the sack.

As I lay there I thought about my friends, or lack of them. I wondered how many of them really cared anything about me, as long as they could party. I seemed to be seeing life from a new perspective. Now I was deeply concerned for my thoughts and actions. As a child, I had been taught the difference between right and wrong, but for the first time in years, doing wrong bothered me. My drinking and dope smoking began bothering my conscience.

On the following day I confronted Dave with what I had experienced. "Dave, the weirdest thing has been happening to me. I think I'm cracking up. Last night at my party I felt so uncomfortable doing what I used to enjoy. I just couldn't be myself. What do you think's wrong with me?"

"Praise the Lord! God is already busy making you into a new creature in Christ. You see, Christ won't come to live in your heart unless you ask forgiveness and desire to change into the person God wants you to be. That's what happened when you prayed over a month ago. Now God is busy changing you into the image of His Son. Just remember one thing. You have a free will. God won't force you into anything. He'll only bring His thoughts into your mind. The decision is up to you. If you listen, His voice becomes clearer. If you don't listen, His voice will grow more distant until you can hardly hear Him. At this point you can either ask forgiveness and start over, or choose to stay that way and be very distant from God."

His words sounded strange, but somehow I knew he was right. I began to fill Dave in on my experiences of the last several months. I told him all about my unexpected release and of the new feelings and emotions going through my heart, mind, and body from the first moment we had started working together. This seemed strange to me because I never had especially cared for him before. He would talk by the hour about God's goodness and grace. I seemed to have a tremendous hunger for his words. Soon, I would even interrupt him with a "Praise the Lord" or "Amen." The words would roll off my tongue. They sounded far-out to my ears, since they were used to a vastly different vocabulary. I asked him question after question. At first they were easy for him to answer, but soon they became more difficult. Dave was right. I was being transformed into an entirely different person.

Dave and I started reading the Bible on a regular basis. It impressed me that many times I would feel a needed change in my life, only to read later that was precisely what God wanted me to do. Dave would encourage me, "Rob, that's a further indication that the Holy Spirit is working in your life." If only every Christian could have at least one Dave in his/ her life! One day Dave compared me to Peter in that I was big, hard-headed, and self-assured. I thought it was fantastic that I reminded him of one of the greatest men in the Bible. That night I read all about Peter in the Gospels. Even though I am not worthy of being mentioned in the same breath, I did recognize definite similarities. In fact, I believe every person, if he studies enough, will see himself mirrored in at least one biblical personality.

As I read the account of Peter's life, it hit me like a load of concrete. My biggest similarity was stubborn, obstinate pride. Christ had to humble Peter before "The Big Fisherman" could be used. For the first time I began to understand God's purpose for allowing me to mess up my career. He had brought me to the point where cocky, self-assured Rob could no longer rely on himself. I had to rely on Him for His strength. I thought about that verse, "Pride goeth before destruction and a haughty spirit before a fall"(Prov. 16:18). Even as many Bible characters were rejected by their peers, I began to experience the same rejection, even by close "friends." One night after a shift, I returned to the apartment. Bill and I had one bedroom with two beds, so I prepared for bed quietly as possible. Evidently I woke him up. He rolled over and began talking. I felt he was stalling as he tried to express himself. After fifteen minutes of idle chatter, he came to the heart of the matter.

"Rob, it's plain you're not the same guy you used to be. You don't like to drink or smoke dope or anything I like to do. Man, you used to be loads of fun. You're the last person I would've thought would turn to religion. You were so cool, Man. I guess that Deacon Dave is rubbing off on you. Well, that's fine, but just promise me one thing. Don't change into a street preacher. I'm already taking some heat for still living here. If people find out I'm living with a Jesus freak, I'll never hear the end of it. Just try not to embarrass me in front of my friends."

"OK, I'll try not to embarrass you, but I wasn't aware that you or our friends found me offensive. I hope you don't think I'm rejecting you. I'm just very thankful to God for delivering me from a jail sentence. I don't drink anymore because it's wrong for me. I'm sorry if you took it wrong. I'll try not to let my new life-style get in your way."

As I fell asleep I nursed hurt feelings that Bill and my old friends were pulling away from me. About a week later Bill moved out. I guess I continued to embarrass him, but I could no more change back into the person he wanted me to be, than he could change into the person I wanted him to be. When he left, most of the other squad members quit coming over. My Barnabas ("Encourager"), Dave, was there to bolster me through this period. We became "soul friends," and this lessened my pain as my old buddies left me.

Dave and I began sharing Christ with others. Many began coming to a Bible study we had started in the barracks. At first only a handful came, but as the weeks passed and people saw that this "Jesus thing" wasn't wearing off, we would have a crowd. Of course, there were scoffers, but almost all of them respected us for our life-style. We tried to be model troops and urged others to do the same. We had shiny boots and pressed uniforms. We even memorized duty assignments. Many other airmen began to follow Dave and me. After a few months, more than twenty men had invited Jesus into their lives. And the witness multiplied as they, too, began to share the Lord with those around them. We had an honest-to-goodness revival going. Sure, many people, including those in Investigations, thought all of this was a cover-up, an effort to free myself of any charges still hanging over my head. Our Bible study group continued to grow in numbers. As part of my personal growth in the Lord, I began to concentrate more on what He thought than what others felt.

A well-known comedian used to chant in his routine: "Strange things are happening!" And they were in my life. One night while we were on duty, Satan was bitten by one of the largest water moccasins I had ever seen. I rushed Satan to the vet who said, "He'll be fine," but he wasn't. He died a few weeks later of a heart problem. He was replaced by Princess, the only female dog at the kennels. I thought it was curious that before I recommitted my life to the Lord, my dog was named Satan. I wondered if it were only a coincidence that when I lived like the devil, my dog's name was Satan.

One night at guard mount, I was telling Kerry, a security policeman, about Christ's love for him. Right at the time he was about to ask Christ into his heart, guard mount broke, and we had to go to our respective posts. That night mine was in the alert area. This area contained B-52s loaded with nuclear weapons. The planes and pilots were ready at a moment's notice to take off and deliver more firepower than both of the prior World Wars had seen together. So it was a highly protected area.

Approximately sixteen security policemen and four K-9 handlers were assigned each night. We handlers were assigned to guard the perimeters. Security personnel in trucks watched over the individual aircraft. Of all the men who could have been assigned to the post next to mine, Kerry was it.

As a military man, my first priority was to protect my post with my dog and fully loaded M-16. But as a Christian, I felt my first priority was to share the gospel. I wrestled with this balance until I decided that my Christian duty even came before my duty as an airman (only later did I discover that my first duty to God was being a good soldier). I waited a few hours for the area to quiet down for the night. Kerry's post was approximately seventy-five yards from mine. I started walking toward him, leading Princess with me. I stopped. How could I possibly leave my post? What if the flight sergeant were to come? Investigations would have me in jail so fast my head would spin. I thought about my dilemma for a moment. I had an idea. I fell down on my knees.

"God, I need Your help. Kerry is very close to accepting Your Son as his Savior. I want to walk over and talk to him about it, but I can't leave my post. Lord, this sounds crazy, but would you please send an angel to watch my post while I'm gone? I'll be back as soon as I can. Please protect Kerry and me as we speak. In Jesus' name I pray. Amen."

I began walking toward Kerry's post. I turned around half expecting to behold an angel behind me. I saw nothing, but I somehow felt he was there. I pitied any intruder who would try to gain access now. My angel would make it difficult for him. Now I could see Kerry on the opposite side of his aircraft. As I waited, He started walking in my direction around his post.

No one was allowed inside the area unless officially OKed by the Aircraft Commander. We were authorized to shoot if anyone tried to gain unauthorized entry. So he was being careful not to step over the line. As he rounded the front of his post, he spotted me, immediately fell down on one knee, and pulled his weapon off his shoulder, putting it in front of him in the upright position. He was prepared to meet force with force.

"Who goes there?" he yelled.

"Kerry, it's me, Rob. Be quiet."

"Oh no, Man, get back to your post before we both go to jail!"

"I will in just a minute, but before I go, I need to tell you about something I feel is so important that I'm willing to take the risk—Jesus Christ and how you stand with Him."

Soon he was completely enthralled with my plain witness. He asked several questions as the minutes passed. Finally I asked the all-important question.

"Kerry, do you feel you're ready to accept Jesus Christ as your Lord and Savior? This means that you'll have to ask forgiveness for your sins and be willing to let God change you into the man He wants you to be. Think about it. It's not an easy decision to make."

He turned it over in his mind and, with a big smile, answered, "Yes, I'm ready!"

"OK, let's pray," I replied hastily, aware that every second counted.

Both of us knelt right there. All of a sudden a pair of lights swung past us across the flight line. It was a Security Police truck! The driver was about 200 yards away from our area, heading right for us. I had read a Scripture that day about using Christ's name against the devil, so without even thinking about it, I stood up and pointed toward the truck, which was speedily closing in on us.

"Satan, I rebuke you in the name of Jesus Christ. You have no power here. God, thank You for Your power that You've given to Your children."

As soon as I finished, an emergency call for the Duty Officer came across the radio. He was requested at CSC immediately. His truck swerved to the right—toward CSC. Kerry almost keeled over. I have to admit I was also surprised. People who had known me would have thought I was stark, raving mad. Who would have thought I had rebuked the devil? I thanked the Lord then and there.

"Oh no, that was the Flight Officer, Captain Maddox. He could've caught us red-handed," Kerry blurted out shakily. We had heard Maddox was the rank-hungriest officer around. We felt he might have arrested his mother if it would mean a promotion.

Kerry and I picked up where we had left off. "Yes, I'm ready to become a Christian now," he said, bowing his head. On our knees I helped him pray a prayer I led. As soon as we finished, I promised we would talk the next day about his new life in Christ.

When I reached my post, a base truck was parked to the side. Its lights were shining in my direction, and I would have to walk directly in front of them. I felt nauseous, as I had a thousand times recently, but this time at least I felt sick for the Lord's sake. I absolutely knew the driver would see me. Once again I prayed for God's protection—then I started walking. I was in the lights for perhaps four seconds. I walked hurriedly the rest of the way to my post. I had made it, but did they see me? No sooner than I was on my post the truck started toward me, pulling up in front of me.

"Who goes there?" I asked.

"Sergeant Black," came a gruff voice.

"Code word?"

"Blue Knight."

"Come ahead."

Sergeant Black pulled up next to me. "How are you tonight, Airman Bryant?"

"Fine, Sir, how are you?"

"All right. Tell me what kind of games you're playing with your dog."

"Games?"

"Yes, games. Why have you been walking without your dog? I've been watching you from over there for the past few minutes, and that's what you were doing. Why, Airman?"

"Well, I, ah, you see, I, ah . . ."

"I don't want to know, Bryant. Just be careful with that dog. Don't let her get away from you anymore. Do you understand me, Airman?"

"Yes sir," I gasped as he pulled away. I waited until he had crossed the alert area; then I went to the next post to talk with the Security guard.

"Hey, Baltic, what in the world was he talking about? What did he mean walking without my dog?"

"I didn't know what he was talking about. He made some comment about you walking without your dog. I looked over, and I didn't see anyone at all. I think he's cracking up. I watched you walk off your post about a half hour ago. And then just now, you passed in front of his lights to get back to your post. Not only is he blind, but he's also seeing things. Maybe he needs some sleep. These long nights can do strange things to your mind."

I returned to my post when it hit me. *You big dummy, don't you get it? The person Black saw walking on your post was the angel you prayed for!* I was overwhelmed and overflowing with a sense of God's providence.

But, the more I thought about it, I knew it was wrong for me to leave my post. I had broken regulations in trying to serve God. I began to feel God would want me to follow the rules, even though Kerry accepted Christ as a result of my little side trip. I later discussed it with Dave, and he told me I was wrong in what I did. I'll never forget his next statement.

"God will protect a person in his ignorance, but once a truth is

learned, he's held accountable." The statement was simple but true. He
showed me a parable which explained the whole circumstance. The explanation for the story was: to whom much is given, of them much will be
required (see Luke 12:48). So the more I learned, the more I was going to
have to be responsible. I thought about that for quite a while. Word
spread concerning the incident on my post. Of course, the good old boys
in Investigations heard about it and decided my "walking on post without my dog" couldn't be used as any kind of evidence. Can you imagine
the judge's face when Roberts would report he wanted to prosecute me
for leaving my post? His evidence: a guardian angel was sent to guard it
for me while I was away!

Our Bible study flourished with a few more than twenty attending.
Several more also received Christ. God continued to teach me valuable
truths. Dave and I could no longer meet the group's spiritual needs and
answer all of their questions. We mulled over the situation for a long
time. We prayed for a person well versed in the Scriptures who could
help bear the load of counseling and teaching. And then the obvious answer lit up in my brain. We were missing the influence of a church. Dave
and I began to pray that the Lord would lead us and our Bible study
group in the direction of a spiritual church . . .

5
In the Market for a Church

It sounds picky considering the kind of life I had been living until recently—Dave and I began fanning out into the area . . . looking for the "right church." Finally, we found it—Ridgelea West Baptist.

After we decided to attend the church, it seemed like a month waiting for the Sunday services to arrive. I wasn't disappointed. The church was beyond my wildest dreams. Ridgelea West was all I had been searching for. The members of of the church were so friendly and warm, I felt as if I had known them all my life. The singing and preaching were spirited and satisfied all I had anticipated. Then I beheld an event I hadn't seen since the age of seven at camp. At the end of the pastor's message, he presented an invitation for people to record their decisions publicly. The congregation was invited for several reasons—to make a profession of faith, that is, to confess Christ as Savior; join the church on "transfer of membership" from another church; be baptized into the membership of the church; make another kind of decision public; or simply to come forward for prayer or counseling.

I knew this was the church I was going to join. The next weekend I was going home on leave, so I decided to join when I came back.

On the very next Sunday, I went forward during the invitation to join the church. The pastor explained that I needed to be baptized. I told him I had been christened. He explained the difference to me. On the following Sunday during the evening worship service I was baptized. This publicly proclaimed the most joyous, fulfilling relationship I have ever enjoyed—between the dear Lord and me. I shared Christ with many of my Air Force buddies. I invited many of them to my new church home, and a number of them accepted Christ and followed Christ in baptism.

Because of the excitement I was experiencing, Deacon Dave became curious, began attending, and eventually joined. You might suspicion that I began to feel ashamed about not sharing my Christian experiences with Mom and Dad. Now that I was baptized, I could no longer stifle my feelings. My parents and I sent cassette tapes back and forth in order to save on long-distance phone calls. I gradually slipped my testimony into the tapes. In a while I was letting it all "hang out." Mom and Dad concurred with me until I talked with them about baptism. I spoke with Mom about the importance of being baptized after a decision to accept Christ as Lord and Savior. She didn't accept that point of view until the Lord broke through to her several years later

Ridgelea West had Sunday School (called Bible Study in some churches) preceding the morning worship service. I began to attend both on a regular basis. It was fantastic to study the Bible with other young adults. One morning a beautiful girl sat beside me and began to chat. I had seen her around the church before and had heard her as well. With her gorgeous voice she had sung in Sunday School and the worship services. It was "tingly" talking with such a uniquely attractive young lady. All seemed to proceed well until we broke up into small groups later on. The fascinating lady and I were in the same group. This turned out to be unfortunate for me. When we were alone at the beginning of Sunday School our discussion was fun, but with other people around the situation took a turn for the worse. I made one of my "cute" comments, and she turned around and leered at me.

"If you wanted to impress the girls by being a big shot and wearing your uniform, maybe you should have wiped the dog hairs off first!"

I looked at her in disbelief. She surely had changed from a moment ago. That was some Dr. Jekyll and Miss Hyde impersonation. I gazed down at the dog hairs. I had come right to church from the kennels, so I had not changed clothes. I wanted to croak from embarrassment. I decided two things. The next time I attended church, I was going to change before showing up, and I was also going to avoid this girl at all costs. She was injurious to one's self-confidence. After church I was a little hurt, but I figured you can't please everybody.

Two weeks later, after the evening worship service, Dr. Jekyll was having a party at her house. I almost collapsed when she went out of her way to invite me. Only to seem friendly, I accepted. Maybe I could leave early anyway. What I didn't know is that a diabolically clever trap had been set for me. Everyone arrived around eight o'clock. Miss Hyde, alias Wanice Lane, was so nice to me and everyone else that I wondered: *Is this the same sarcastic girl I met in Sunday School?* I also met her parents, terrific people. I hit it off with them from the word go. Around nine o'clock, everyone started leaving. It seemed strange that everyone would leave so soon, but I also prepared to say good-night. Wanice met me as I was leaving.

"Rob, would you like to stay and have some coffee? I wish you would. I need to talk with you."

"Yeah, I'd like that," I replied, looking down to make sure there were no dog hairs on my clothes. Soon we were drinking coffee in the living room. Out of the clear blue she interrupted me in the middle of a sentence.

"Rob, I'm so sorry about what I said to you in Sunday School. I've regretted it ever since. I guess I just wanted so badly to talk with you that I said the first thing that came to my mind, and it came out all wrong. I must confess it bothered me when some of the other girls were staring at you as you talked. Please forgive me."

"Sure, Wanice. I didn't take it personally anyway. Think nothing of it," I answered, knowing I was lying. She had hurt me, but it no longer seemed to matter. As I looked into her deep blue eyes, I could read a complete sincerity. I was becoming captive to those eyes. I didn't mind this kind of captivity, though. At around ten o'clock, I reluctantly left.

To reciprocate I asked her to a Bible study at my house. I also invited several biblically "savvy" people from the church, who might be able to slake my insatiable thirst for spiritual answers. Most of the people, sensing how many questions I would ask, brought huge Bibles, concordances, different translations, and commentaries. By seven o'clock we were already studying. I kidded them about locking the doors until they had satisfactorily answered all of my questions. I was only half-kidding.

Somewhere in the study, we were reading from the Book of 1 Timothy about godly relationships with others. I looked up from my Bible to contemplate what was being read. And I gazed directly across the room into Wanice's azure eyes. We searched each other's eyes for what seemed like an eternity. Through our eyes in that instant, I believe we exchanged more feeling and understanding than many couples do in a lifetime. No words were necessary to convey the fact that I was looking into the eyes of my wife-to-be.

I was somewhat fidgety around Wanice, because in times past I had struggled with my sexual feelings around such a beautiful woman. As it turned out I had nothing to worry about. God turned me into the perfect gentleman.

During the next month, Wanice and I knit our souls and spirits together. On May 19, while sitting by a duck pond, I proposed to her. You know what her answer was. I wanted not to "waltz across Texas" but to run and leap nonstop clear across the Lone Star State. I notified Mom and Dad immediately. Wanice and I would plan to fly home so they could meet their future daughter-in-law. They were a somewhat concerned about the length of our relationship before the engagement. I had to admit that six weeks was a short period, but we were both confident of our decision.

We would fly home in July. I called my parents to schedule the best time for us all. The dates were set and we readied ourselves for the trip. Like nearly all brides-to-be, Wanice was a little shaky about meeting her future in-laws for the first time, but she handled it in her usual sweet manner.

Upon arriving in New York, we were greeted with the usual hugs and kisses. But Mom and Dad had undergone a tempestuous divorce, so Wanice and I saw them separately. After visiting with both sides of the family for several days, Wanice and I visited the two churches involved in my family's separate lives.

On the following Sunday night, Wanice and I conducted the service at the church where Dad belonged. As though an angel were singing through her, Wanice sang some of the most heavenly songs I have ever heard. About halfway through the service, I gave my testimony about what Christ had done for my life. That church was usually rather quiet during its services. Most of the time there would be only an occasional "Amen." This time, though, there was an outburst of praise. People were actually shouting: "Praise God, Hallelujah, Thank You Jesus," and the like.

Just about ten minutes into my testimony, in walked my mom, my little brother, and a few old friends of mine. I about fell over. I introduced them to the congregation right then and there. After I had completed my message, I gave—you guessed it—an invitation. My father and stepmother came forward to share how they had seen me change over the years. A young boy came forward to trust Jesus as his Savior. To this day I praise God for his salvation.

My dad and his wife began to grow in their Christian faith. Today they are a joy to be around. My stepbrother also received the Lord into his life. Later on, my little brother became a member of the family of faith. My mom is active in an evangelical church. Now remarried, she goes to church with her stepchildren. My stepsisters were baptized not long ago. My older brother was not present, but today he has a family, and they all have a commitment to Jesus Christ. As a matter of fact, Danny, his oldest son, has become a constant source of encouragement to me in recent years. He would become a prayer warrior for me in the biggest ordeal of my entire life. We are all of different denominations, but thanks to God, the question at the judgment seat of Christ will not be which local church we belonged to, but Who is in our heart. I'm glad that I was willing to be a fisher of persons. I will see my whole family in heaven because of it.

6
One Last Shot

When Wanice and I returned from New York, I decided to move back into the Security Police barracks. This would save me about 200 dollars a month. Wanice and I were hoping to save enough for a luxury honeymoon, now only three months away. I didn't enjoy the idea of living in the barracks again. There was so little privacy. Every self-respecting Security Policeman owned an expensive stereo so powerful it could change the moon's orbit with sound waves.

But I also wanted the opportunity to share Christ with the guys who worked on different flights. I reported to the Barracks Sergeant for my room assignment. He informed me that there was only one room open— 336. I was about to ask who my roommate was, when the Sergeant was called away to another duty.

Looking like a pack mule, soon I was standing in front of my barracks room. Awkwardly pulling my key from my pocket, I opened the door and walked in. The occupant let out an audible gasp as I entered.

"Oh, I'm sorry. I didn't mean to scare you," I apologized as I turned around . . . and looked into the face of a man who was turning white as a sheet. *Matt Walker!*

"OK, Rob, let's just stay calm here. If you'll go back out the way you came, I promise I won't call Law Enforcement. But if you touch me, I'll have you behind bars this time," he sputtered, a look of terror in his eyes.

"Relax, Matt, I'm going to be your new roommate. I'm not here to hurt you. You know I've changed. I wouldn't lay a hand on you."

"I don't care how much you've changed. You're not staying here. I'll talk to the Barracks Sergeant."

He moved toward the door, and I did nifty steps to get out of his way. He edged around me carefully, never removing his eyes from me. He backed out of the room and dashed down the hall. This was wild—only one room open and it had to be his! I prayed for guidance. I began to feel that maybe this was God's mysterious plan. In about an hour Matt came back. He had a scared yet frustrated look on his face. "Look, I don't know how you pulled this, but as soon as possible I'm going to move. And remember if I turn up dead it will be pretty obvious who did it."

I couldn't repress my laughter. "Look, Matt, I'm serious, I didn't create this room arrangement. I wouldn't hurt you for anything. Look, Guy, I'm a new creature in Christ. Think about it, Matt. Why would I want to do something stupid and find myself right back in the same mess I was in? Believe me, you're as safe as if you were living with a lamb."

"Yeah, but lambs don't threaten to kill people," he replied, as he lay down on his bunk.

There was no convincing him. He watched my every move like a hawk. We worked on different squads so when I would come in he would be asleep. As soon as I would come in, no matter how quiet I would be, he would sit up and watch me. He would not sleep after I came in. He lived with me for three weeks before I came in to find that he had moved, but during that time he saw I was a different person in a way that he could never have seen otherwise.

Work remained about the same. I tried to be a model soldier and witness to as many as I could. Now that I was living in the barracks, I could follow up on some of the contacts I made at work. Investigations remained quiet. Other than some surprise searches in the barracks and at the kennels, I never saw Roberts. But I knew he was still watching. It seemed like most of the searches were on the third floor of the barracks or on my shift at work. K-9 handlers were sometimes known to have drug habits, so naturally Law Enforcement kept a close eye on us. I stuck out in the ranks because of my changed life-style, but that didn't stop Roberts.

Soon after, I returned from my vacation. Dave had been moved to a different squad. One night while I was reading the Bible, it dawned on me why God had split us up. Now we were strong enough to go out on our own. We had learned all we needed from each other. God had put us together for a purpose, and that was to grow as Christians. We were now to the point that God was going to lead us in different directions. We had no idea that the directions He was leading us in were so different until a few weeks later.

Dave was working the midnight shift at the kennels, when suddenly he realized that he could not see. He was completely blind. I mean 100-percent, total-darkness blind. He was relieved of duty and then examined by local doctors. They had never seen this particular phenomenon, so they sent him to a large military hospital on another base. He was diagnosed there as having a rare eye disease. He was released from the Security Police and was taking eye tests when his vision partially returned. He could not carry a gun with his current eyesight, so he underwent a battery of Air Force tests for an alternate career field. He "aced" all of the tests and was cross-trained into Air Force Intelligence. This is one of the most sought-after career fields. God used a seeming disaster to bless Dave's life. I would learn later that God uses tragedy to make us grow as Christians. Just as metal is purified by fire, so are we. In the years to follow, Dave would re-enlist and be transferred to the other side of the world. Yes, he was even "tortured" by being sent to Hawaii for four years. God led Dave in another direction, but we are still very close to this day.

With only a month until my marriage, I had saved as much money as I could. In fact, I saved seventy-five dollars with which I bought a diamond ring for Wanice. This ring was so big, that if using a magnifying glass, one could almost see it on top of the four gold prongs!

Most of my efforts were toward preparing myself for marriage so I barely noticed that a new K-9 handler was added to the ranks and put on my squad. He was a very likable fellow named Max. He was so interested in other people, always asking questions and wanting to spend time with his friends. He chose some odd friends, though. It seemed that he couldn't be around about six of us enough. The friends he chose were the wild party animals who drank and used as many drugs as they could scrounge up. On the other hand he chose good old, clean-living Rob as his closest friend, yet he drank and did drugs with his other friends. He just put on the personality of the group he was with. This made me uncomfortable around him. He was too curious about matters that were none of his business.

One night while Max and his buddies were partying, they were raided by Law Enforcement, and he singlehandedly fought the officers at the door, allowing all of his friends to escape. He even took a severe beating by one of the officers because he wouldn't come across with the names of the other dopers. He became an instant hero. Everyone treated him like a king. His buddies threw a big party for him. After the party, he led an assault on the officer's club with two of his friends. They waited until it closed in order to steal beer. They were both caught, but somehow Max narrowly escaped. This guy lived at light speed all of the time. He was constantly partying yet he still had time to buddy-buddy with me. One night we were on post together talking.

"Rob, I tell you, some of the guys I hang around think they are really tough and smart, but I'm a shrewd judge of character. I know tough and smart when I see it. They can't hold a candle to you in that department. I mean, from what I hear, you really burned a whole bunch of officers, and security people, and got away with it. I bet I've heard the story a million times how you stole the ammo. Man, now that is tough and smart. I heard that you were going to kill Walker over it, too. You just don't realize how many of the guys look up to you. You are the last of a dying breed. And just between the two of us, I know this Jesus thing is just a coverup. It's brilliant. Even if they took you to a court-martial, who would believe the prosecution when you are living like a saint? That was a nice touch. You really outsmarted them. Would you do me the honor of telling me the story from your own mouth? I'm sure that I didn't hear the whole story. You probably got away with even more than everyone thinks. I want to hear how you got away with it. You might be able to teach me a thing or two."

He had boosted my ego so much I was almost proud of what I had done. But the Lord brought me back to earth with His still small voice that I was becoming accustomed to hearing. I felt as if I should not speak with Max about it. I figured there could only be two reasons God would not want me to share my testimony with the guy. One, God did not want to save him, and that wasn't consistent with the Scriptures. Or two, God was protecting me somehow. This seemed more likely. So I refrained from saying anything. He seemed disappointed but he wasn't discouraged. He hounded me almost daily for the real story. I tried to stay away from him.

Finally the big day came. Wanice and I were married on September 4, 1976. We spent our honeymoon at a nearby motel because both of us had to return to work in three days. My fears were put to rest that simply because I was marrying a Christian girl, that she would be a cold lover. She was exactly the opposite. For the first time we were totally free to be to each other what we wanted to be. I discovered that making love as Christians was better than sex. This love was not shrouded with games and guilt.

We moved into an apartment near the base. After returning to the base, I discovered that Max and his friend Ace had been caught selling some drugs on the base, but that once again Max narrowly escaped. Now we all knew that Investigations had been after Ace for a long time. He was the biggest drug dealer on the base. He wore diamonds, drove a Cadillac, spent money like water, and received good treatment from some of the officers who were clients. He walked around the base like King Tut. I knew he wasn't going to take this lying down. He told several of the other men that he had been set up by someone and that when he found out who, they were dead. No one doubted his words.

In the meantime Max was still running around causing trouble everywhere he went. He seemed to drive people to do things they wanted to do, but do it in such a way that they would get caught. One day Max didn't show up for work. He was gone. About twenty of us were called suddenly to Investigations. We were informed that most of us were going to be relieved of duty until further notice with various pending charges, most of them drug-related. I was informed that Max, alias Captain Stevens, an undercover agent for the OSI, had gathered additional information on my case, and I would be notified when he was returning in order to testify against me in my hearing. I couldn't believe my ears. I had gotten married, all was going well, I thought, and yet it seemed I was prison bound again. All of the other men that were called over to Investigations were mad and screaming about how they were going to get even. Ace and I had the most serious charges against us. He appeared to be very calm. Soon after I heard him talking to a friend.

"I've got everything under control. Now that I know who my enemy is, I know what to do. I ain't going to no jail house. They ain't going to have any evidence on me very shortly. You just watch."

The following week, we were all informed that the charges were being dropped. No explanation was given for their sudden change of plans. A few days later Sergeant Vincent told us he had heard from Investigations that Captain Stevens had been shot. Although we never heard any specific details, Stevens had been shot between the eyes by a professional at his next assignment. I was sure God protected me. Sergeant Roberts's plan had failed once again. He was soon transferred to another base.

My last year in the military went by speedily. I was quick to tell others what God had done in my life and could do in theirs. On August 15, 1977, I received an honorable discharge from the Air Force. Both the Air Force and I were all too glad to part. At last I was out of Roberts's hands completely. However, two years after my discharge the Air Force completely remodeled the on-base nuclear site and closed down altogether the off-base site. Today the on-base site is very secure.

7
My Climb to the Top

I hit college like a whirlwind. I attended school full-time for two years, and took over 100 hours. This included a geological trip to the Teton Mountains in Wyoming. I began working two jobs to pay expenses after the birth of our first son.

However, my thirst for money caused me to shirk many duties as a husband, father, and Christian. I felt I was much too busy to attend church as much as I had in the past. I soon lost the joy of worshipping the Lord. My relationship with the Lord was cooling quickly. In order to escape the situation for a few days and rethink my goals, I bought two tickets to Hawaii for Wanice and me. Not only could we see the islands, but I could again see Dave Koksma, who had been transferred to the Islands. Dave could tell I was different but little was spoken about it. But Dave's desire to serve the Lord was frustrating to me since my relationship to the Lord had grown so cold. To this day my wishywashi-ness of the past embarrasses me.

When we returned from Hawaii, I moved from job to job. I was turning into a quitter. On July 1, 1981, I went to work for Pengo Industries, an oil service company. I was hired to work the three-to-eleven shift in one of the many stockrooms. I made two decisions as I started to work for Pengo. One—I was not going to quit. Two—I was going to climb to the top of this organization no matter what it required. The stockroom was a mess. I worked on the night shift alone while there were four men on the day shift. I decided that I was going to outwork all of them in order to be noticed. On several occasions I brought upper-level management's attention to problems in the stockroom by correcting the problem and sounding a brass band over my accomplishments. Instead of giving the credit to my boss or making him look good, I was always drawing attention to myself. This plan accomplished many things. Besides being disliked by my fellow workers, the stockroom improved in appearance and I was able to upgrade the system that was being used. Last but not least, I was promoted into another division of Pengo. My bosses in the stockroom were more than willing to let me go. They knew that if I weren't promoted soon, I might try to steal their jobs.

My new job entailed writing technical manuals. These manuals were to discuss the use, operation, and maintenance of various tools. After writing several manuals and talking with men who worked in the oil fields, I discovered that the real money was in actual oilfield work.

Keeping my ears open for any need of a person with my talents in a field position with Pengo, I began practicing logging techniques with the oil-well tools. Part of my job was to run the equipment and then write the operating instructions, so I was already familiar with most of them. Within a few months, I was proficient at running all the analog and most of the digital systems. I felt comfortable with all of the electronics, oscilloscopes, recorders, modules, and panels. Soon the technicians at our test well were becoming dependent on my knowledge of tool operations.

I felt I was ready to make the move. One day I heard of an opening in Giddings, Texas. I went home and told Wanice all about it. In no uncertain terms she laid down the law: she absolutely did not want to move to a small town. I could understand that, so I grudgingly backed off. A few weeks later an opening appeared in Abilene, Texas. Again I told Wanice all about this assignment—and that this was not in a small town. Next, she decided she did not want to live in West Texas. I wasn't as understanding this time, but I backed off again. The next opening was in Oklahoma City.

I've got her, I thought. *It's not a small town, and it's not in West Texas.* This time she protested that it was too far from home. I wasn't understanding this time. I blew my top.

"Wanice, what do you want? This is the third time I've tried to persuade you to move to a great job opportunity for me. And three times you've found different things wrong with the area. I don't believe that the area has anything to do with your negative responses. Now tell me why you really don't want to move." I knew I had her. She couldn't possibly answer this with a good reason. I simply wanted to show her that she was not willing to follow her husband if it meant moving away from her family. She had lived in Fort Worth all her life and had a multitude of friends and family there. I stood there with a "Gotcha Look" on my face and waited for her answer.

"Rob, if you answer this question with a 'yes,' I will follow you gladly anywhere you lead me. Don't just say 'yes' quickly; think about it. Have you prayed about this move, and do you feel like God wants us to move? There was a time not so long ago that you would not do anything before praying about it. Where is that man? I haven't seen him in quite awhile. I would follow that man anywhere. I'm not saying that I won't go with you, but if you want me to trust you and be happy by your side, I've got to know."

I was dumbfounded. She had completely caught me off guard with the truth. The truth of the matter was that I had not even considered praying about the decision. She was correct. A few years ago, I would have been on my knees in prayer about such a big decision. I was not the same man anymore, but in order to save face I had a hasty answer. "Why would God mind me making more money? We can still go to church and worship the Lord in Oklahoma." She agreed with that, and I prayed a perfunctory prayer about the assignment. A few days later the position was filled by someone else before I could give my answer to the district manager. I was so frustrated about missing out on the job that I decided that regardless of where the next assignment was, I was going to take it.

About a month later, I heard of an opening in Southern California. I talked with the president of that subsidiary. He said I sounded like the man he wanted and that I had the job. I went home and told Wanice we were moving. We put the house on the market and two weeks later I was on my way to Ventura, California. Wanice stayed behind to sell the house. This would give me several weeks to find a house out there and settle in. I kissed Wanice and Jason good-bye and drove for two days to arrive there. This left Wanice all alone with a two-year-old, four months pregnant with another one, and without a car, but she didn't say a word.

On my first day of work, one of the field hands invited me to live with him and his roommate. I accepted. During the two days I stayed there I saw all ten of the commandments broken. I didn't want to go to jail just because I happened to be in the same room with these guys, so I moved into one of the wireline station's bathrooms. It wasn't home, but it was sufficient. In the meantime the company put me right to work. During the first month I went out on almost every job they had. I would get up at 3:30 AM, warm up the huge wireline trucks, make sure everything was loaded, and leave with the other men around five for the oil well. After the job was through, I would return to the station around dark, eat a quick meal, and go to bed.

During the first few weeks, I was trained as a rigger and engineer which meant that I worked with all of the high-pressure equipment in order to allow the tools to be lowered into the oil well. Then I would clean all of the oil off my face and hands, climb up into the truck, and do the engineering work. This entailed sending various electronic tools into the well and interpreting the recording, pulses, and analog signals. I loved my work and I was very good at it. One day while on a job, I told one of the operators who was assigned to me to do a particular thing. He turned to me and said "No," standing his ground with clenched fists. He waited for my response. I was standing up above him in the door of the wireline truck. He stood there smiling and said, "Make me."

At first I was not sure what to do but I knew if this behavior went unchecked, I would command no respect from my subordinates. Our station had some tough characters; their unspoken motto was, "The one who can fight, is the one who is right." So I felt I had to establish my authority on their terms. One of the other men was standing nearby watching what was taking place. I felt I had but one recourse. I dove out of the truck on top of him hitting him twice in the face. The fight was over. He wanted no part of my large arms pushing my fists at him. He backed off and said that he would get it done right away. Of course, later he told the other men that I had caught him off guard and "he would get me next time." The next time never came, and I didn't have any more direct confrontations challenging my authority. On the other hand, now I was respected for being big, not for being a Christian. I knew I was wrong and that now witnessing to them, if I ever got around to it, would be very difficult.

One night soon after, I was heating up my supper late at night at the shop. I looked in a mirror as I passed by on the way to the stove. What I saw was so shocking that I walked back for a closer look. My face was completely covered with oil, my hair was matted with dirt and grease, my eyes were bloodshot, and I looked old and tired. It was if suddenly I saw for the first time what condition I was in. What had happened to me? Here I was heating up a can of stew on a small stove, filthy from head to toe. I was living at the station and sleeping in a bathroom. I had no close friends and I had left my pregnant wife and son at home. What bothered me even more was that I was no longer a witnessing Christian. I thought back over the last five years since getting out of the service. My career was taking an upward swing, but personally, I was on the way down. I wasn't smoking, drinking, cursing, or acting immoral in any way, but I knew I was distant from God just the same. Each time I prayed it was as if my prayers were bouncing off a brick wall. I ate my dinner and went to sleep considering my condition.

Two weeks later my wife called and told me that our house had sold. By this time I had saved enough for a rental house, so I rented a condominium in Camarillo, California. Two days later I was on a plane bound for home. We had been separated for just over six weeks.

When I stepped off the plane, Wanice, Jason, and I exchanged hugs and kisses for fifteen minutes. I broke the news to her that we had to be back in four days. On the following day we loaded up the truck, had a small party with our friends. We hit the road the next morning. The drive to California took three long hot days in a U-Haul. Jason loved every minute of it. But for a five-month pregnant woman, it was an ordeal. She never complained, though. I knew where she got her strength. I was a little envious of her relationship with the Lord. When we arrived, a few of my work friends helped me unpack my furniture. Next morning I was back at work, which meant Wanice had to do most of the unpacking.

The days passed quickly since I was working twelve to sixteen hours a day with very few days off. When I didn't have to work on Sunday, I would visit churches with Wanice. We tried two or three. One Sunday morning we walked into Pleasant Valley Baptist Church and we both knew we had found our church home. On the following Sunday we joined. Everyone was so friendly. We made several friends right away. When I had time off during the evenings, we got together with several of them. It was during this short time that I would establish friendships that would soon help carry me through the toughest time in my life.

I loved my job even though it was hot and dirty work. Gradually my bosses worked me into the engineering position I was hired for. This meant that I did not have to rig as much. I rarely complained when they put me on back-to-back logging jobs. There were only two logging engineers and the other engineer could not log with all of the cased hole and production logging tools, so they heavily depended on me. They told me constantly how they appreciated my work and gave me a company truck to drive.

One day while on a perforating job with high powered explosives, my crew and I set up all of our equipment and waited for the well service crew to arrive so that we could begin. When they arrived we were all ready to drop our gun in the well and perforate. The tool pusher (the man who was in charge of the well service unit) walked over to me.

"Didn't you guys hear? We don't need you until after lunch."

"No, the last thing I heard was to be here at daybreak. We are ready to set up the pressure equipment and blow holes in this well."

"Well, I just talked with the company engineer and he said we needed to pull the tubing out of the well before you can begin."

"We noticed that a joint of tubing was still in the well and that the pipe tally in the rack was small, but we got ready anyway just in case," I said to the tool pusher.

"Come back around twelve and we'll be ready for you."

"OK, see you around lunchtime," I replied.

I told my crew to secure the gun and move our small equipment out of the way so the well crew could go to work. We drove our pickup back down the mountain to a small town to eat and relax for a few hours. After eating we drove around for awhile. Around 11 AM, we started back up the mountain. Just as we arrived at the base of the hill, an ambulance shot by us. It was going up the mountain. On any given day there were several well locations that were being serviced, so we didn't give it much thought. It was driving faster than us but we could see it up ahead. There were over fifty small roads on the mountain. But it was taking all of the right turns to go to our site. I started to sweat a little.

"Does anyone remember grounding the perforating gun," I asked quietly. Everyone looked at each other. All I heard in return was the three of them saying "I thought you did" to each other.

Suddenly it grew very quiet in the cab. We all knew that if that gun had gone off hurting or killing someone, one of us was going to jail on manslaughter charges. I knew that the someone was me, since I was in charge. We all also knew that if the gun had gone off that it would spray thirty-six shots of molten metal. The shrapnel would go in every direction, with each single jet much stronger than several shot guns. The ambulance continued on a path to our site. Finally only one more intersection was left for him to choose. We all held our breath waiting to see if he it turned toward our well site. As we rounded the corner, we saw it head right toward our site. It was over. I was going to jail and worse, someone or several people were either badly hurt, dying, or dead. I stepped on the accelerator and everyone held on as we flew down the narrow dirt road with a cliff to the left. We arrived at the location approximately three minutes after the ambulance. As soon as we pulled up the company representative ran over to our truck and stuck his finger right in my face.

"You get that gun off my location right now."

"Let's go," I shouted to the men. We all jumped out of the truck and ran toward the perforator. When we got closer I could see that the gun had not fired and that it was grounded. It was so natural to ground the gun that one of the men had done it without even thinking. I could also see Adrian, one of the well service crew members, lying in a crumpled mass at the base of the rig. At that point we knew we had another problem to face. I never had to say another word. They were trained to react to emergencies such as this. Two of the men grabbed one end, one grabbed the middle and I grabbed the other end of the gun. I pointed down the road from which we had come. We ran as fast as we could carrying the four-hundred-pound, twenty-four-foot gun at our sides. We knew we had just a few more seconds before a helicopter would be coming to pick up our friend. We heard the helicopter prop before we saw it. The sound echoed off the walls of the canyons. Then we saw it. It came flying over the valley right toward us. We knew that if the helicopter were to use his radio, or transfer static with the flying debris, or even fly directly overhead, the gun could go off. "OK, that's far enough," I yelled. "Drop it on three. One, Two, Three." We dropped the gun together and I turned to the man who had been on the end of the gun.

"Ground it, then get away," I yelled. "Here it comes."

He pulled a piece of wire out of his pocket, spliced it to the feed-through wire, and taped it to the gun. He was up on his feet in less then twenty seconds. He joined us at a location that was out of danger. The helicopter flew right over the gun thirty seconds after we had left it. It was grounded properly. Thank God it didn't go off. The paramedics landed and had poor Adrian on the stretcher in about five minutes. He had fallen off the rig. He had landed on his back, catching his arms and legs beneath him. We could hear him scream. One of his pant legs was torn with the bone jutting from his leg and both of his arms were broken in several places. The helicopter took Adrian to the local hospital. For several minutes none of us could speak. The events of the past fifteen minutes were more than I could handle standing up. The accident had such a impact on me that I wandered around the site for a few minutes getting my wits about me. The company engineer told us to take the rest of the day off.

That night, I told Wanice all about the accident. It scared her that the same thing could happen to me. It made me very safety conscious. It also made me think about my fading relationship with the Lord. I knew that He could not bless disobedience. But I just couldn't make the commitment to Him that I knew He wanted.

8
... and Great Was the Fall

Despite only four hours of sleep, I climbed out of bed at 4:30 AM sharp. Soon I had loaded my truck with all of the equipment I needed for the day's work, everything except the radioactive fluid I used to gather the well's flow percentages and other pertinent information. The truck's motor was dead. I panicked. I had to drive to the office, pick up the radioactive fluid, meet my crew, and then drive to Santa Maria over two hours away. I called the office, and asked one of the men to swing by and pick me up. He arrived twenty minutes later. We transferred all of the equipment into his vehicle and drove to the office. With equipment and crew we then left for Santa Maria. We were over an hour late by then, and we raced to the well location, deep inside Cat Canyon. Little did I know that these difficulties were only the beginning of my sorrows.

My crew began setting up the equipment, while I loaded the radioactive fluid into the temperature/tracer ejector. I tested the rest of my electrical equipment which was designed to ascertain the production rates, fluid movement, casing integrity, the gradient and differential temperature, formation content, casing and tubing leaks, and more. Within an hour, we were ready to go into the well. My operator opened the well rams, and I began slowly lowering the testing tools into the well. I turned on the equipment, ran a few passes, when suddenly the tool shorted out.

We brought it up and worked on it for over an hour, but it was no use. It was dead. I replaced it with the backup tool, ran a few more logs, and then it too shorted out. I couldn't believe it. We tried repairing the second tool. It too was beyond field repair, despite several hours of attempts. I decided to call it quits for the day, to repair the tool back at the shop. We left all of the equipment where it was and made the two-hour drive back. Upon arriving, we repaired the tool properly. After loading the truck, I left for home. It was after 8 PM when I arrived, tired and disgusted.

By 7 AM we were back on location at Cat Canyon. The date was December 10, 1982. I was hoping our luck had changed when we started into the well. But just then, the cable that lowered the tools down into the well jumped out of its pulley on top of the portable mast truck. We were sunk. The mast could not be laid down because the cable was fed through a tall piece of pressure equipment. The well was under pressure so we couldn't remove the pressure equipment. The company representative was growing impatient and did not want to stop injection into the well, which left only one course of action. One of us had to go to the top of the mast unit and put the cable back into the pulley. This was not a particularly dangerous task. I had done it many times.

The three of us on the job discussed all our options. The safest and fastest way to correct the problem was to go up. The question was: who would go? I reluctantly volunteered since I had the most experience. I very carefully secured the lifting device around my hips. One of the other men ran the wench that lifted me high into the air. Within minutes I was fifty feet up and directly across from the pulley to be fixed. The wench man stopped lifting me at my command. I reached out to try to fix the pulley. The cable could not be forced back into the sleeve. Try as I might, it wouldn't go. I decided to remove the sleeve and take it down with me. Unfastening it, I put it in my lap. Suddenly I felt a jerk. I looked up at the pulley that was holding me. It was tilting sideways at a funny angle. Looking down, I saw how high fifty feet really was. I realized the danger I was in and decided that I wanted down quickly. I called for the hoist man. He walked over to let me down.

"OK, you can let me down now, but go slow. This pulley up here looks strange, it might not . . ." I felt another jerk, only this time I wasn't stopping.

"Oh Lord, I'm falling!" I yelled. "Somebody help me." I saw the ground rushing up to me. I remember praying that God would let me die. I knew I was going to be hurt badly. Well, He didn't, and I was. I fell in the sitting position. I hit the ground on my rear. I felt as if I had been hit by a truck from behind. My back and head were next. They slammed down on the ground. I felt my back break with a crunch and my head hit something, causing my helmet to fly off of my head. My ears rang with the sound of the impact and cracking bones. I felt a tremendously painful sensation in the middle of my back as if someone had stuck a knife into it. I never lost consciousness.

Everyone came running over to me. Suddenly I realized that I could not feel anything from my lower abdomen down. I spit out broken teeth and blood. Blood ran down the side of my head into my ear. Breathing was very difficult, as the pain in my back restricted my air intake. With every gasp my back hurt worse. Slowly my reasoning returned to me, and I looked around. It all had happened so suddenly that the employees were just now to me. Directly over my chest was an iron fence that ran around the wellhead. That is what I had hit my head on. I was thankful that I had been wearing my helmet. The fence could have broken my neck or caved my head in. Looking directly up, I saw something that still has not been explained. My body was not lying directly beneath the broken pulley. I was approximately eight feet over to the right of the well head. Had I fallen straight down, I could have been impaled on the pressure equipment. My thoughts were fairly clear considering what had just taken place, but nearby voices were distant and distorted, as if I were in a tunnel.

As the minutes crawled by, the pain in my back intensified. Someone had called the hospital. In the meantime I tried to move my legs. It was no use; they would not respond. I could turn my head slowly although I could not lift it. I could move my fingers, but my arms felt too heavy to lift. I looked over at Dave, one of the operators. He was looking at me with unbelief in his eyes. Slowly the shock of the fall dissipated and the grim reality of the situation began to sink in. I was over an hour away from the nearest hospital. I could not feel or move from the waist down.

"Oh, dear Lord, my back is broken," I moaned out loud.

"Rob, the paramedics are coming. Just hold on. You're going to make it."

"Dave, what do I look like? I can't feel my legs. Are they still there?"

"Yes, they are there. I'm not going to lie to you. Your left foot is bent sideways. It's probably broken, but the rest of you looks OK. How do you feel?"

"Like I've just fallen fifty feet," I said, trying to laugh. Laughing caused a severe pain to shoot through my entire abdomen. I stopped right away. My insides felt torn up. After a few more minutes of gasping for air I prayed out loud. "Dear God, help me! I'm not going to make it." Suddenly breathing was easier but the pain grew worse. It seemed like hours, but minutes later I could hear a siren. At first it was distant, but it rang louder and louder until it pulled up on location, and several trained paramedics were all around me. The leader was tremendously proficient. By asking me a few questions, he knew what must be done and the probable extent of my injuries. His voice was much clearer than Dave's had been minutes before. "What is your name?" he asked, looking into my face.

"Rob."

"Rob what?"

"Rob Bryant."

"Where are you?"

"On a well site running," I took several breaths, "a production log."

"Where do you hurt?"

"My back."

"Can you feel your legs?"

"No."

"Can you turn your head and move your fingers?"

"Yes," I said, showing him.

"OK, just lie perfectly still. We are going to put you on a stretcher and prepare you for a helicopter."

"Please be careful. I feel as if I'm broken in two."

"Trust me. You are going to be OK. Just breathe slow and easy. You've got the best paramedic team in the county. Try to relax."

They began removing the chain that was wrapped around my hips. My boots were cut off and my pants were slit up the sides with a knife. I was lying in some water and for the first time, the sixty-degree air and steady breeze began to make me shiver. Every vibration hurt my back, and I was becoming sick in my stomach. I prayed that I would not cough or vomit.

Before I knew it, they had applied a splint to my broken ankle and had put me on a stretcher. They put a sheet over me which helped me retain some body heat. I was awed at their efficiency, and if I wasn't in so much pain, I would have told them. Talking was quickly becoming too much of a strain on my back and lung capacity. I lay there at their complete mercy.

"Please, God, kill me. I can't stand any more pain," I whispered. One of the paramedics heard me.

"I don't want to hear any more talk like that. You're doing really well. You can make it. Don't give up."

"Can you knock me out with a pain killer?" I asked, gasping for air. "Listen to me carefully," he returned, "right now we are not sure how badly you are hurt. Your head is bleeding, and you might have internal bleeding. If we were to give you some sort of anesthesia it might hurt you more than do good. Hold on. You are really doing well." *Doing well. Who is he trying to kid?* I thought. I wondered if I *were* dying. The thought of never seeing Wanice, Jason, and the baby to be helped me hang on. I wasn't ready to die.

"God, if I live, I'll get my life straightened out," I whispered.

The pain grew worse. I began moaning with every breath. I just couldn't get enough air. I lost consciousness for about five seconds, but the immense pain revived me. I had heard of people dying of pain. Now I could believe it.

Off in the distance, I heard the sound of a helicopter. Within seconds the pilot was looking for a place to land. He was directed by one of the paramedics. Debris filled the air. I slowly turned my head away from the wind, but I was still breathing dirt. I closed my eyes. Suddenly I felt myself being lifted. As the stretcher was lifted off the ground, I felt a release of pressure to my broken vertebrae which gave me a momentary relief of pain. They quickly carried me to the helicopter and found it was difficult putting me into the copter. "Take the door off," the pilot yelled over the roar of the engine and prop.

"This will be just like Nam," he yelled at me with a smile. If he was trying to make me feel at ease, it wasn't working. They removed the door and shoved it in behind me. One of the paramedics jumped in with me and away we went. The sound was deafening. The added G-force exerted on my body as we took off almost made me pass out. Suddenly I found it almost impossible to breath. Air was rushing into the chopper at an incredible speed, forming a near-vacuum around my face. Each breath was almost impossible, but I refused to give up. I fought the fear of suffocating.

"Oh God, help me," I prayed. I took in one breath at a time, not worrying about the next. I prayed for strength for the next breath. The paramedic glanced over, saw me struggling for air, and cupped his hands over my face, thus allowing me to breath freely again. I was close to shock. A torrent of cold air was racing in across my wet body. I was freezing. Each shiver agonized my back beyond words. I wondered why I hadn't passed out by this time. I felt cheated of unconsciousness.

Several minutes later, we landed at the Santa Maria hospital. All I remember about the landing was all of the hands that pulled me from the chopper. The paramedic briefed the doctor on my condition. In the background I heard voices saying, "Grab this" and "Stabilize that," as we raced across the parking lot. I was carried carefully and smoothly into the emergency room and set down on a table. As soon as my swollen vertebrae hit the table, I screamed with pain. The side of my head was then shaved and sewed up as I answered questions about my pain and paralysis. By now I was screaming with each breath. One nurse asked me questions about my wife and son to make sure they were not losing me. In the background I heard somebody say, "Fifty feet. My God, I wonder what his insides are like." I was in too much pain to worry about dying. I relished the thought.

From there I was taken to X-Ray. I was placed on the table face up. The hard table relentlessly pushed up against my broken back. *"How much pain can a person take?"* I wondered. For the first time since the accident, I cried. I found out later that my broken vertebrae were pushing out almost through the skin. The X-Ray still makes me shudder. After several X-Rays of my back and skull, I was told to wait to see if they were going to develop properly.

"I'm not going anywhere," I jokingly told the X-Ray technician through the tears. Finally after an excruciating twenty minutes on the X-Ray table, I heard the magic words.

"Mr. Bryant, I'm about to administer you an anesthetic. This should relieve you of the . . ." Those would be the last clear words I would hear for over a week. I had been conscious for over five hours. They were undoubtedly the longest, most excruciating five hours of my life.

In the meantime, Wanice was notified of my accident. She was cleaning house when the phone rang.

"Hello, Wanice, this is Jim Clemans. Rob has been hurt. We don't know how badly yet. I am sending one of the men to pick you up and bring you here to the office. Rob has been taken to the hospital."

Wanice left Jason with a neighbor and a truck picked her up a few minutes later. She was taken to the office where Mike and Jim were waiting. The three of them rushed to the hospital over two hours away. Wanice figured that the accident must have been major as Mike and Jim did not want to talk about it. All she could think about was Adrian and how badly he had been hurt. Little did she know that my injuries were much worse. All she was told was that I had fallen and that I was hurt. She was not told the extent of my injury. She waited for over an hour in the waiting room for a report. Finally the doctor came out of the emergency room to talk with her.

"Mrs. Bryant, at this point we don't know how serious your husband's injuries are. We do know that he has a broken back and ankle. He is experiencing paralysis from the waist down. What we are most concerned about now is to control any internal bleeding. We do not hear any bowel sounds which is rather serious also. At this point we have no way of telling how much damage has been done to his spinal cord. If it is not bad, he will experience almost total return of his leg movement. If it is badly damaged, the paralysis may be permanent. I have scheduled a surgery tomorrow morning for your husband. I am going to straighten his backbone, insert two steel rods on each side of his vertebrae and fuse it all together. The next forty-eight hours will tell us how seriously he has been hurt. I don't believe in pulling any punches. I feel I have an obligation to tell you the truth. I hope I have not shocked you."

Of course, she was in shock about the whole thing. That morning her husband had gone to work as a healthy muscular man. Now, several hours later, he was fighting for his health and quite possibly his life. She sat down, now eight months pregnant, and was near a breakdown. But after a few minutes an incredible peace swept through her. God's Spirit told her that I was in God's hands and that everything was all right.

That afternoon and evening the doctor prepared me for surgery. The hospital was not fully prepared for major neurological surgery, so the doctor set up a radio in the operating room to talk to Rancho Los Amigos (a neurological and spinal rehabilitation hospital) in Downey, California. He didn't feel totally confident in this kind of surgery. Rancho thought it was wise to fly me to them, but my doctor wanted to try. The full extent of his inexperience with this kind of surgery would not be realized until six months later. My back surgery was scheduled for six o'clock in the morning. After being put under anesthesia, they placed me in a room for the night for observation and cleanup. Try as they might, they could not remove all of the mud, grease, and oil from my face and hair. One of my fellow employees, John Allen, came up to see me and used good old grease remover on me as I slept.

At six the next morning, the planned five-hour surgery began. It was not over until 3 PM, nine hours later. Wanice and a few of my work mates came to be with me during the surgery, but I didn't reach semi-consciousness for several days. The only thing I remember from the first week is occasionally waking to Wanice's sweet voice telling me everything was going to be OK.

Meanwhile, several of our friends in Fort Worth, Texas, were having a party. Wanice called them and they each talked with her and encouraged her. We were told later that several at the party broke down and cried after her call. They decided to send one of Wanice's closest friends out to be with her. They took up a collection (some of the people who gave money did not even know me) from my Sunday School class. They collected enough to fly Jane Hurst out to California. Jane was a Godsend for Wanice. They both cried together. Wanice and Jane spent hours at the hospital watching over me and praying. Even though they were in the same room with me, my mind was miles away.

I opened my eyes and saw I was in bed. I seemed to be floating. I couldn't feel anything. I felt as if I was levitating over the bed. Just then a nurse walked into the recovery room. She had a very pleasant look on her face as she walked over to the side of my bed.

"How are you feeling?" she asked me with a compassionate look on her face. Her voice sounded like it was coming from a tunnel. It was distant and distorted.

"Well, I can't seem to feel anything," I returned.

She walked to the foot of my bed and pulled the covers back.

"I'm going to make the pain go away. In just a moment, you won't feel any more pain."

She reached into her smock pocket and suddenly the pleasant look on her face began to turn into a twisted smile. Slowly she began pulling something from her pocket. At first all I could see was a black handle, but the more she pulled her hand out I could make out what it was. She pulled out the largest butcher knife I had ever seen. She lifted it high.

"Nooo!" I cried.

She brought down the knife and buried it deep into my right thigh. She began thrusting the knife over and over into my legs. Blood flew everywhere. She threw the covers off and charged up toward the top of my bed. Suddenly, she was gone. Everything was gone.

The darkness was the thickest black I had ever expereinced. Slowly, the darkness dissipated into a dull grey. I began to be able to make out sounds. "Beep. Beep. Beep." I could hear voices off in the distance. Slowly I could see the forms of people standing around me. My eyes focused on the shape closest to me. It was a doctor. He was wrapping me with wet strips of white bandages. He was winding them completely around me. He appeared to be making a mummy out of me. *Was this another dream?* I couldn't move, lift my arms or talk. I looked around the room. I was surrounded by equipment that was beeping and blinking. A tube ran up my bed and disappeared into my nose which then ran down into my stomach. My throat was raw from trying to swallow with the tube in it.

My mouth was so dry that I would have killed for a drink of cool water. Another tube ran up the bed which catheritized me. There were several electrode monitors placed on various parts of my body. A large intravenous bag was suspended over my bed with a tube that ran down to a needle in my left arm. The doctor continued to wrap me with the long wet strips of cloth. By now I could see that he was making a plaster cast around my upper body. It was from my lower waist up to my arm pits. I was being suspended above my bed by some sort of apparatus which allowed the doctor to wrap the strips all the way around me. The tube up my nose and down my throat and the drugs which sedated me prevented me from talking. One of the nurses produced a needle and gave me a shot in my rear. Slowly I faded out again. The morphine she had given me killed the pain and pushed me back into unconsciousness. The dream about the nurse with the knife did not return. However, it was replaced with other hallucinations which were just as terrifying.

I faded in and out of consciousness. I was painfully aware of the body jacket that I would wear for the next three months. It was hard, difficult to breath in, and hurt my back. Slowly, I was weaned off the stronger drugs and my dreams lessened in their severity, but my back pain grew worse. Sleeping became impossible in the plaster body jacket. I could not move because of its size and weight. About every four hours I was rolled to a new position. All of the positions hurt after just a few minutes. I thought the pain and mental torture would drive me mad.

On the tenth day, I was moved from intensive care to a semi-private room which was not occupied. Because of my hallucinations, paranoia, and constant screams during the night caused by the pain, they thought it best if I were by myself. This made my situation worse. Now I had no one to talk to. Wanice could not travel much in her condition, so she visited about every third day. I felt as if I had been abandoned by God, Wanice, and my fellow workers. As a matter of fact, with exception of John Allen and Dave Teston, not one of my fellow workers ever bothered to come and see me. Slowly the drugs and pain decreased. I began to think more clearly, although I resisted calling relatives or friends because of the deep depression I was in. Slowly the shock of the accident passed and I was left with the grim reality of the situation. I was a paraplegic.

Now that I was becoming aware of my surroundings the body jacket was even a bigger problem. I was sliding down into it. My raw back was sliding across the rough interior and the jacket began to rub against the incision. I told several of the nurses it was bothering me, but they were so used to my screams they just thought I was complaining about something new.

Fifteen days after my accident, it was Christmas day. Wanice brought Jason with her to see me. It was the first time that I could remember seeing him since the accident. Jason couldn't understand at all why I couldn't walk. He wanted me to come down on the floor and play with his toys. Jason got on my nerves very quickly and our visit was cut short. I was very short and cross with Jason and Wanice. Several of my other friends from church stopped in, but I just didn't want their company for very long.

Jason was becoming a holy terror at home. He wanted his Daddy to come home. Without me there to discipline him, Wanice was in a losing battle. When Jason did visit me, he would study me as if I were a stranger. He soon learned that I wasn't strong enough to spank him and could not chase him. He became disobedient and confused about the whole thing. His world had changed forever, and he knew it.

On December 31, Wanice made her final trip to see me before she was going to leave me to fly home to Texas to have our second child. It was the most difficult separation we had ever known. She did not want to leave me all alone in California, and I needed her so badly. A couple from our church, Bob and Ruthie Peterson, brought her up to Santa Maria. They had no idea what to say to us to ease our agony. They just wanted to be there for moral support. The three of them visited with me for a couple of hours. When it was time for them to go, I asked one of the nurses if I could be transferred to a wheelchair to escort them to the door. The nurse had to get the doctor's permission because I had not yet been released from the prone position. The doctor allowed me to take a short trip in the wheelchair.

After a twenty-minute struggle, I was in the chair. This new position made me sick to my stomach and I thought that my back was breaking but I knew I had something important to do. I insisted on pushing the wheelchair on my own. The four of us went downstairs. As we were on our way to the door, we passed the room that I had been told about; it was a chapel.

"Wanice, Bob, Ruthie, I have some business to take care of in the chapel. Would you like to join me?" The four of us entered from the back. It was beautiful. There were stained-glass windows and an ornately covered altar in the center. We went up to the front pew and everyone sat down.

By now my back was killing me but I knew what I was about to do was more important than the pain. I turned to my guests.

"I need to talk to the Lord, and I want you to be here. Let's pray," I said as we all bowed our heads. It grew very quiet. "God, I just want to thank You for getting my attention. I don't know if You caused my accident or just allowed it to happen or what. But if this is what it takes for me to be Your servant, then it is all worth it. I've been growing more distant from You over the last five years. I'm ready to come home. I want to thank You for the pain, the accident, and everything I am about to endure through this trial. I want You to make me into a choice servant through all of this. I also want You to make this into a blessing somehow. And someday I want to do something through all of this that will cause others to look to You in their time of need. Please watch over Wanice and Jason during their trip home. I pray that You will help Wanice in the delivery and give us a healthy child. In Jesus' name I pray, Amen."

After I finished, it was deathly quiet. The only sounds were Wanice's muffled sobs. During those seconds a miracle happened. All of my bitterness disappeared. Within seconds the bitterness that some people live with for years or a lifetime, vanished. I would still have occasional bouts with depression but the bitterness was gone forever. I had complete faith that God had heard my prayer. It was the first time in a long while that I knew my prayer would be answered. I was one with God again. I relished in the communion. Even though my back was hurting beyond words, I was comforted inside where the lasting pain would have been. Bob and Ruthie began to cry with Wanice. We all left the chapel and I rolled to the door to say good-bye to Wanice, Bob, and Ruthie. We all cried as the moment was too heavy to bear for all of us. They waved good-bye, and I went back to my room. But I wasn't alone. God was by my side.

On the following day the chaplain came to see me. I told him about my life prior to the accident, about the accident and my prayer. I'll never forget his words to me.

"When a person becomes a Christian, he is like a nugget of gold. As the trials of life come along they are like fire. Fire has an unusual relationship with gold. Instead of burning or destroying the gold, it purifies it. It can also be molded into a different shape. It becomes pliable and much more precious than before. A lost man is like a piece of metal. As the fire is applied to it, it becomes hard. After being heated up several times it becomes brittle and will break. Have you ever noticed there are two types of old people? On one hand, some are jolly and friendly. The others are cold and bitter. The difference is that the first group has learned to allow hard times to mold them into better people. The other people grow more bitter with each trial.

"The Book of James says that we should count it all blessing when we are tried, because it develops us into a more usable person by the Lord. God can use this to make you into a better person. Also remember that if you seek the Kingdom of God and His righteousness, He will help us through our earthly problems. You know people say that the Bible says that all things work together for good. That is not what it says. It says that all things work together for good *to those who love Him and who are called according to His purpose.* God can make this into a blessing if you seek Him out. If I understood you a moment ago, when you were telling me of your life before the accident, you were a Christian and a churchgo-er, but you forgot something very important. The Old Testament says that you shall "have no other gods before Me." In the New Testament it says that you should not lose your first love. When you think about it, your first love is your God. It sounds like you made your climb to the top your first love and put God second. He wants to be number one in your life. I am excited to see what God is going to do through your life now that He is in the driver's seat again."

We had a short prayer together. I thought about his words for a long time. I thought back through the prior five years and saw that I had left my first love. I knew that I had walked away from God. I didn't believe God was punishing me for disobedience but He cannot bless disobedi-ence either. Well, I was going to change my direction. I wanted to be right square in the middle of His will from that moment on.

I marveled at the priest's wisdom. I could have taken what he said in the wrong spirit, but if I had, I would have missed his point anyway. I knew that the words he spoke to me were sent from God. We saw a lot of each other during the following two weeks. He was just what the doctor ordered. For what good is a strong body with a weak spirit?

Just after Wanice left, I called Jim Hurst, a friend in my Sunday School class back in Texas. We talked for awhile and then I said the words that would change my life.

"Jim, whatever it takes, I am going to walk back into my Sunday School class. I know that it is impossible, but just you watch. God is in the business of doing the impossible. I don't know when I'll be coming home, but when I do, God and I are going to do it."

He said "OK," but I could tell he was just trying to be nice. God was going to use Jim in a big way in my life from that moment on. If someone would have told either one of us what would happen in the months to come, we would have thought they were crazy.

On January 6, I was flown to Downey, California, in a small care flight. It was there that I would undergo four months of rehabilitation. Now that my condition was stabilized and I was healing, there was nothing else the hospital at Santa Maria could do for me. The trip was very painful. I felt every pocket in the air and every bump on the road, but I made it. My brother Mike and Mom spent the next week there with me, waiting to start my physical therapy. I was so glad that they had come. I would have been very lonely waiting around for news from Wanice about our second child. The rooms did not have phones, so I arranged to have one put in on the big day. The hours crept by. I had hoped that I could have started my therapy right away to keep my mind occupied. I felt so left out knowing that Wanice was having our baby so far away and I couldn't do anything to comfort or help her. It bothered me that I had to hear about it by phone instead of being there. It also bothered me that I would not see the baby for two weeks after its birth. Everyone was there but me.

Slowly the days passed and January 10 arrived. At nine o'clock my phone rang. My stomach was up in my throat. *Had everything gone OK? Was Wanice all right? Was my baby healthy?* I answered the phone.

"Hello, Wanice, is that you?"

"Yes," came a tired weak voice from the other end. "I wouldn't let them put me out until I could tell you in person what we have. Rob, we have the most precious little boy you've have ever seen. He's so beautiful andhealthy, and I'm OK—just a little tired and sore. I love you, Rob. I can't wait to see you and show you our little boy, Jonathan. I've got to go now. See you soon."

"I love you too, Wanice. I'm grateful to God that you and the baby are fine. Thanks for being so strong," I said, not sure if she heard or understood me in her condition. She handed the phone to her mother and we talked for awhile. After she hung up I was so excited, even though it still bothered me that I could not be there.

At ten o'clock Ruthie Peterson and Judy Wilson, two women from our church, walked in my room to celebrate with me about my child. I told them that Wanice had already called and told them all of the news. I tried to hide my frustrations and was fairly successful. They were just as excited about the birth of my son as I was. They hung a little sign over my bed that congratulated me on the birth of my son. Judy and Ruthie and their husbands were becoming regular visitors of mine and we were growing very close. We talked and prayed together for awhile. We thanked God for His grace in giving me a healthy child. I tried to be as cheerful and thankful as I could, but it wasn't working. Finally, knowing that I wasn't fooling them with my mask, I broke down and cried. They cried right along with me. It was during those moments that we grew even closer. They were God-sent to be with me during that time. Little did I know that in the next few minutes they would be comforting me for a very different reason.

(Top) Airman First Class Rob G. Bryant, then twenty, put his patrol dog "Satan" through his paces. (Bottom) Satan was at the end of his leash out in the field (U. S. Air Force Photos).

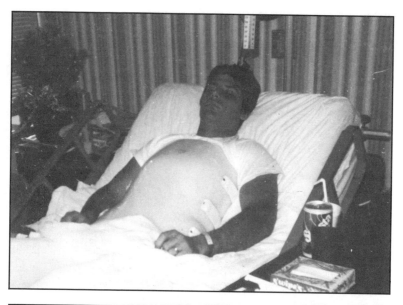

(Top) The situation was dim after Rob fell fifty feet from an oil rig. Here he was in a full body cast. (Bottom) Rob celebrated Valentine's Day with wife Wanice (left) and friend Ruthie Peterson during rehabilitation at Rancho Los Amigos.

(Top) Wanice Bryant (center) and dear friends Ruthie Peterson and Judy Wilson, with their prayers and support, helped Rob make it through rehab. (Bottom) After rehab, there was rejoicing on Rob's first day back at Southcliff. Wanice was holding their second born, Jonathan.

It's been uphill for Rob Bryant . . . but he's made it. Here he was accompanied by Jason, then four years old (Photo by Jay Racz).

(Top) "It's good to be back home again." (Bottom) Romping with Jason, Wanice, and Jonathan at home.

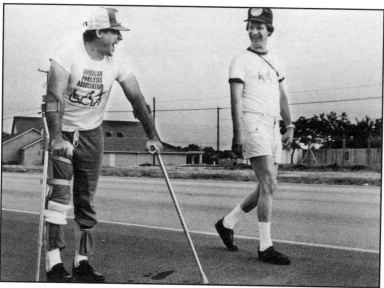

(Top) Training for "The Miracle Walk" (twenty-four miles from Fort Worth to Dallas, Texas) meant excruciating, torturous pain. (Bottom) Jeff Wilson urged Rob to "Go, Go, Go!" (Photos by Jay Racz).

(Top) Rob, Bob Peterson (center), and Jeff Wilson, his buddies in training, stopped for a break between arduous workouts. (Bottom) Rob beams with satisfaction during "The Miracle Walk" (Photos by Jay Racz).

Victory at last! (Photo by Jay Racz).

(Top) The Bryants at home in Fort Worth—Wanice, Jason, Jonathan, and Rob, all rarin' to go on a nationwide Row Cycle trip of over 3,000 miles! (Bottom) Rob in his Row Cycle, in training once again. He will be accompanied by his brother Steve and Steve's wife, Kristi.

9
"You'll Never Walk Again!"

While Ruthie and Judy were still in the room, a young doctor came in. "Excuse me, Ladies, but I need to speak with Mr. Bryant for about ten minutes. You can just wait in the hall," he said politely.

"We'll be right back, Rob," Ruthie said on her way out of the room. After they left, the doctor closed the door and turned to me. "May I call you Rob?"

"Certainly."

"Well, Rob, I just wanted to welcome you to Rancho Los Amigos. It is a standard practice for a staff doctor to examine incoming patients to ascertain the neurological damage level. In this way we can best help you with your rehabilitation. I am going to ask you some questions and perform some simple tests. First, can you move either of your legs at all?"

"No."

"Try. Can you lift them, roll them, move a toe or anything?"

"I can't, but I'll try," I said as I began trying to move my legs. I was about to turn blue with effort when he finally stopped me.

"OK. That answers the question of movement. Now let's test your sensation level. Let's try what is fondly called the pizza cutter test."

"What in the world is the pizza cutter test," I asked curiously?

"This should answer your question," he said reaching into his smock pocket. He pulled out an instrument that really did look like a pizza cutter except that instead of a cutting edge it had tiny spurs.

"What are you going to do with that?" I asked hoping that my suspicions were wrong.

"I need to know where the sensation level begins in order to make an estimate of the severity of your paralysis."

Before I could say anything about it, he started pushing the pizza cutter over my left leg. He started with my right foot and then proceeded up my calf, past the knee and onto my upper thigh. I could see the white dimples that it left on my skin. They would disappear after just a second. *Can I feel it? Will it hurt?* My questions were soon answered. Finally he got to my lower waist and I yelled, "I can feel it now."

He stopped the test and wrote some notes on his clipboard. "OK, that was very good. Now let's try the other leg."

What does he mean by "good"? I wondered. He repeated the process on the other leg until he got to my lower left abdomen. "OK, I can feel it now," I yelled again.

He wrote a few more notes and then noticed for the first time the sign that the girls had made concerning Jonathan's birth. "A boy, huh? That's great," he said as he paused, as if he had something more to say.

"I have something to tell you, but I'm not sure that this is the time."

"Go ahead, Doctor. I think I know what you are going to say."

"What I am about to tell you is not an absolute truth, but it is a strong indication of what you should expect." He paused for a second. "Do you remember taking the sensation test two days after your accident."

"No, did I have one?"

"Yes, I've got a record of it right here. You were probably so sedated that you don't remember. According to this report and judging by the test we just performed, there has been no change in your motor or sensory damage. Today marks one month since the date of your injury. Based on these tests and the fact that there have been no noticeable signs of improvement, I have an obligation to tell you that, in all probability, YOU WILL NEVER WALK AGAIN."

Despite the fact that I anticipated what he was going to say, I was still shocked.

"But the doctor at the Santa Maria Hospital said that there was a chance that my feeling and movement would return," I said in disbelief.

"He was correct, but normally if you are going to have any appreciable return of nerves, it would have already taken place. Each day that passes, the chances of movement or sensation returning are substantially decreased. Statistics tell us that if a person is not moving anything from the waist down after thirty days, he probably never will. Most of the therapy that you will receive here will concern your new life in a wheelchair, not trying to walk again."

His words rang in my ears. Up until that very moment, I really had believed I could almost completely recover. The doctor walked out taking all my hopes with him. A few moments later, Ruthie and Judy walked in laughing and talking about the baby. Neither of them needed a doctor's degree in psychology to tell them that something had just happened to me.

"What's wrong?" Judy asked with a compassionate voice.

I told them what the doctor had said. It grew very quiet for a few seconds until Ruthie suggested that we pray. Each of us prayed in turn and then I closed with this prayer.

"God, I want to reaffirm my life to You again, just as I did just a few days ago in the chapel. I also want to pray that someday I will walk into Sunday School. I believe that You can change things if I pray. I promise if I can walk someday, I will give You all of the glory. Please help me in my time of need. And God, thank You again for my healthy son. In Jesus' name I pray. Amen."

Judy and Ruthie left soon after, but I knew that their prayers were going to remain there with me. Three days later, I was moved into the ward where I would begin my rehabilitation work. My new home for the next three-and-one-half months would be room 518, bed one. Although I was moved a couple of times, I spent the bulk of the time there. The room was approximately twenty-five feet square. It had six beds, three on one side and three on the other. It reminded me of my military days, except for the smell and abundance of hospital equipment. Apparently, my roommates had been here for some time. They had put pictures on the wall and were very possessive about their small living space.

I shared the room with five other men with spinal injuries. During that time Mike, Max, Donnie, Mr. Stewart, and Grant would be my family. We learned to encourage each other and laugh and cry together. My first two days were spent in bed just being introduced to the staff of doctors, physical therapists, occupational therapists, nurses, aides, and other residents like recreational therapists, social psychologists, and a few of the hospital directors. On the very first morning, I met Dr. Comar, the hospital's medical director. We hit it off right away and became close friends. Another person I became very close to was the resident priest. I wasn't Catholic but he didn't care. We had many deep conversations about our faith and lives.

On the morning of January 15, I was supposed to start my physical therapy. I had my first appointment at 10 AM concerning transfer (moving out of the wheelchair onto mats or tables) training. At 7 AM, breakfast was served in bed. I used to think eating in bed was fun, until necessity made it a daily routine. I ate quickly in anticipation of my first day of therapy. One of the nurses aids started helping me dress at 8. All of a sudden, I became violently ill. I vomited all over her and myself. She cleaned me up and we attributed my upset stomach to eating too fast and to nervousness. She started dressing me again when I got sick for the second time. This time she suspected something very different. She disappeared into the hall and came back with the medicine nurse. The nurse looked into my eyes and white face. She knew right away what it was.

"When is the last time you had a bowel movement?" she asked with concern in her voice.

"Oh, I don't know—four or five days," I replied quietly so that new roommates wouldn't know everything about me.

She felt my lower stomach. It was sore and as hard as a rock.

"You are seriously impacted!" she said rushing out of the room.

In a few moments, a doctor returned and examined me more closely.

"Yes, Nurse, he needs a Rancho Special."

"Impacted?" yelled one of my new roommates. "Oh, no, not a Rancho Special," came several cries from around the room.

"Rancho Special? What in the world is that?" I asked.

Without a word, the nurse disappeared again and came back with a little bottle that really did look like a soft drink. I drank it as I was instructed. For the following two days my bowels were emptied chemically with the worst case of diarrhea ever recorded. Now I could understand why my roommates were upset with my condition too. My affliction was very obvious to anyone in the general vicinity. I learned quickly that one of the problems of a spinal injury at my level is that the intestinal muscles no longer work as they did before. I was taught to take care of that aspect of my new life from that moment on. It was also during this period that my internal catheter was removed and I started to wear an external catheter. However, my bladder ceased to function also as a result of the injury. Two months of additional training and time were required before my bladder would function again. This was accomplished by intermittently catheterizing myself every few hours. At first internal catheterization took place every three hours, then four, eight, twelve, twenty-four—until gradually my bladder emptied by itself, although I could no longer control it. These two aspects of my new life seemed small in comparison to my never walking again, but they proved to be an immense problem in the years to come.

It was also during this time that I decided that I was going to work as hard as I could to walk. I was tired of lying there. I decided that the very first thing I was going to do was talk to my physical therapist about walking with braces and crutches. I remembered when I was told I was going to jail. God demonstrated to me that He was able to do the impossible and defy the odds. Being told I was never going to walk again seemed to me to be a similar circumstance. Both of the statements were based on hard facts, but if God could do something about my going to jail, maybe He could do something about this situation. I prayed constantly during the following two days in anticipation of my discussion with my therapist. I really believed that God was going to help me as long as I was prepared to give Him all of the praise and glory. Two days later, I was back to my old self, and ready for my therapy once again.

I was dressed by a nurse in loose clothing over my cumbersome body jacket, including a diaper the size of a small blanket. I felt like Baby Huey. Next a large tarp was placed under me by rolling me from side to side. The nurses moved a small hydraulically powered hoist over to my bed and hooked the loops at each corner of my tarp to the long lifting arm. They slowly pumped the hand lever and suddenly I was up in the air over my bed. Carefully they rolled the hoist away from my bed and positioned me over my wheelchair. I was so frightened that the hoist or tarp would break. I had lost all faith in mechanical means of lifting. But I was lowered slowly and safely into my chair and a seat belt was placed around me. Because I had very weak stomach muscles, I could fall straight forward if stopped suddenly. My body jacket pressed down on my thighs so hard that they started to turn white. I showed the nurses and they said they would have orthotics cut it down a little bit that night. I felt light-headed and sick in my stomach since this was my first time in the chair in over a week. My longest stay in the chair had been one hour. I set my goal that day to stay in the chair for two-and-one-half hours. The nurses thought that my goal was a little unrealistic, but they agreed to let me try. Already my back was hurting but I wasn't going to say a word. I wanted to get to work. I had a goal of walking into Sunday School and I was going to do it.

I rolled over to the sink to shave and brush my teeth. I looked in the mirror and just about scared myself into jumping out of the wheelchair. My hair was a greasy mess, I needed a shave and I looked as white as a ghost. I did what I could but the only thing that would help this mess was a long hot bath. I would soon learn that the hospital was understaffed at night and I would get one or two baths a week. After brushing my hair into an Elvis-Presley-style hairdo, I rolled down the hall to work with my physical therapist for the first time. On the way there, I stopped at the nurses' station and talked with them a minute. They encouraged me to give therapy my full attention. I agreed that I would as I rolled out into the hall and headed for therapy. I soon earned a reputation for being a good patient and I was very well liked by all. Most of the time, the patients who passed through this hospital were not in a terrific mood at the time and consequently made life hard for the nurses. But I had decided that this was my problem not theirs, and I was going to beat this thing.

Upon rolling into the physical-therapy room, I saw many strange pieces of apparatus. The racks, as I would come to call them, had several victims in their clutches. The patients had their legs lifted or spread or seemingly wrapped around their bodies in a knot. Elsewhere people were trying to transfer out of their chairs onto a table of equal height. There were tables with suspended pulleys for leg exercises, for those who could move their legs. A cart with all sizes of dumbbells was in a corner. A rickshaw-looking apparatus was in the middle of the room. Weights were placed behind the patient on the ends of the long sticks with a fulcrum in between. The patient would push down on the sticks so as to work on triceps and chest muscles. At the far end of the room were wall pegs with braces and crutches hanging down. Also at that end was a set of parallel bars with someone trying to walk with braces between the bars. I rolled down to watch him for a minute. I could see right away that he had some voluntary movement of his legs. He could straighten his thigh some, but he had no movement from the knees down. He wore braces on his calves and ankles. *This is what I'll be doing in a couple of weeks*, I told myself. I heard my name being called from behind me. I turned and saw Beth, my physical therapist, sitting on one of the tables waving for me to come over. I rolled over. "Hello again, Rob. How are you feeling?"

"Fine, I'm ready to start therapy."

"Good, the first thing that we are going to try is the transfer from the wheelchair to the mat."

"OK, but later I want to talk to you about trying to walk with braces like that man over there," I said pointing to the man in the parallel bars. She turned and looked at him and then turned back to me. "We'll talk about it later, but I wouldn't count on it. You see he can move his legs. You cannot. I will let you try that in the future if I feel you can. But try to be realistic. Don't build yourself up to be disappointed.

"I've already decided that I am going to walk. Just you wait and see," I said smiling. She turned around and looked at me with a stern look. Evidently she thought I was trying to buck her authority over me. She got red in the face.

"You will do as I say, I am your physical therapist and I will say when you are ready. You are not in control here, I am. Now let's get back to what I said you are going to do. You will transfer from the wheelchair to the mats."

"I didn't mean to make you mad, it's just that I've set a goal to walk. I thought that you would be excited about that. I won't bring it up again."

She regained her composure and handed me a long skinny board to slide on in order to scoot across to the mat. I slipped it under my rear and tried to slide to the mat. The problem was that I couldn't push down enough to lift my rear off the mat because my body jacket would not let me bend. After two or three attempts, I finally made it.

"Now slide back into your chair like this," she said in a dull tone.

She demonstrated how to transfer in the reverse direction. After about fifteen minutes of sweat and effort, I plopped back into my chair. After five weeks of being in bed, my arms were weak and shakey.

"Now do it again," she said as she walked off to help someone else. I was so exhausted and almost out of breath, but I was going to make sure that she saw that I was prepared to work to meet my goal.

"I'll give it my best shot," I told her with determination in my voice. During the following hour, I completed four more transfers. After an hour of transferring, I was to the point of utter exhaustion. I couldn't believe that this little bit of exercise was tiring me. But I didn't give up. I was in the process of trying one last transfer when she returned and said I could go and walked off again. One of the other therapists who had seen how hard I had worked, told me that I had done really well.

"Most people can only do one or two transfers at the most and some people take several visits to transfer once. You really did well. I can see right now that you are going to do well here, if you keep your present attitude."

"Well, thank you, but why didn't Beth tell me that?"

"I'm sure she was just busy. She is a very good therapist. I'm sure you will learn a lot."

"Thanks for the pep talk. I needed it," I said, starting to roll off. We became close friends. I would need a friend because, unintentionally, I had started a war with Beth. I was reminded that when a man of faith set his goals, along would come Satan to try to stop him. I was told several times that Beth was a fine therapist and a fun person, but she never showed that side to me. We both were goal setters and I had set a goal which she felt challenged her authority over me. Regardless of how I would try to please her, I would find I never could.

After leaving the physical therapy room, I rolled around the hospital. I would soon discover that Rancho was on some beautiful land. Almost daily, I would try to retreat to a quiet place on the grounds for prayer and to be alone. Privacy was something to be coveted since I was living with five other people in my room. During these retreats, I went all over the huge hospital. It was a massive place, filled with patients with all manners of problems. I found that there were several wards—one for head trauma, one for stroke victims, two for spinal injuries, one for amputees, and one for assorted diseases. I learned that I was one of the lucky ones as far as the extent of my injuries. If I was tempted to feel sorry for myself, I only needed to look around to regain a proper attitude.

Finally, the two-and-one-half hours in my wheelchair were over and I headed back to my room. By this time my back was hurting badly but I said little about it. I ate sitting up for the first time since my accident now five weeks ago. It felt good. After lunch, I was put to bed with the hydraulic lift. The body jacket had put deep bruises on the top of my legs, so orthotics cut my jacket to fit me properly.

As the first few weeks passed, I was soon able to stay in my chair for increasingly long periods. Soon I was able to tolerate eight hours of continuous sitting. This is when my therapy increased in its ferocity. Now not only was I in a transfer class at nine o'clock, but I was involved in a weight-lifting class, endurance-training class, "wheelie" class, ranging and dressing sessions. Weight lifting consisted of dumbbells and a pulley apparatus to work on the arms and chest. It felt good to work out, but my back pain prohibited an all-out effort on my behalf. I started with a fifteen-pound dumbbell, it felt like fifty. To start with, I could pull sixty pounds with the pulley system. Also in weight-lifting class were the parallel bars. We used them to do parallel bar dips. By placing my feet into a strap that was hung between the bars, I would try to lift my body weight several times. In the beginning, I could raise myself no more than ten times. In transfer class, I was learning how to transfer onto beds, other chairs, into a car, and so forth. Soon I was transferring with little trouble. The body jacket did not allow me to accomplish all of the transfers. I would not learn to transfer into a bathtub or to the floor until the jacket came off six weeks later.

Next, I started on the endurance track. The idea behind this was to increase lung capacity and maintain a strong cardiovascular system. Now that my activities were severely limited, weight gain and the loss of strength would be constant problems. The track was approximately one mile. A physical therapist would time laps around the track and check one's pulse before and after to record any improvement. Because I knew walking was going to be very tiring, I worked extra hard. I began trying to dress myself in the mornings, but I couldn't reach my lower legs or feet until the body jacket came off. Beth came to my room once a day to range my legs. My leg muscles were becoming very tight because of a lack of movement. Ranging consisted of a one-hour torture treatment on the rack to stretch my legs. The ranging was complete, it seemed, when the therapist had wrapped your legs around your head and body four times in a knot.

One of the most depressing aspects of my stay in the hospital were the Dear John speeches that I heard from wives, girlfriends, and family members. I even heard one wife say to her husband, "When I said *for better or worse,* I didn't mean this." She then walked out of his life like a person would walk out of a store after shopping. It occurred to me that possibly Wanice could be having some of the same thoughts. I decided to talk to her and give her a choice. I decided that I loved her enough to let her go if that would make her happier. On her next visit to the hospital, I took her into a private room.

I cleared my throat and thought for a moment before speaking.

"Wanice, it has occurred to me that you may be in a situation that you feel obligated to stick with, but you may not want to go through."

"What do you mean?" she asked with an innocent look.

"I guess what I'm offering you is a one-time proposition. If you feel that you can no longer be my wife, I understand. But, this offer is good for today only. I've got to know now."

"Rob, I love you more now than the day I married you. Besides, in a way, you need me more than you ever have before. That makes me more valuable to you, and therefore, you'll probably love me more. Besides, why do you think I would leave you? You wouldn't leave me, would you?"

"I don't know. I don't want to take your attitude for granted by saying one way or the other what I would do." It was never brought up again.

In my third week of therapy, I was assigned to a new therapist, Sue Robinson. Sue was a student finishing her degree with a six-week internship. We hit it off right away. She was so warm and friendly all the time.

Sue was constantly praising my attitude and hard work. I kept my promise to Beth by not talking about walking, although I wasn't sure why it bothered her so much. My close relationship with Sue seemed to bother Beth also. Sue told me that Beth lectured her on the problems of getting too close to a patient.

"This is a hard business, and we've got to be hard on them to keep them in line. If you get too close, you lose your objectivity. Besides, if we become friendly with all our patients, we could feel sorry for them," she told her.

However, this didn't stop us; we still remained very close. I discussed problems with Sue that I would not feel comfortable speaking about unless she were a friend. Sue also came to the hospital after hours, to play wheelchair basketball with me on her own time. This bothered Beth too, so Sue stopped coming as regularly. Liz, my occupational therapist, told me that one day while discussing my case, Beth suddenly went into a fit of rage and cried that people were being too friendly with me and giving me special treatment. Soon after, when a wheelchair loader was added to the top of my cart, Beth just about bit Liz's head off.

"Why wasn't I consulted about this?" she asked Liz.

"Because it's not your department! Occupational therapy takes care of the car, work and home, and you know it. Why does Rob bother you so much? Everyone else likes him."

Beth stormed off in a rage. In her eyes, war had been declared.

Wanice came to visit with me two or three times a week for four hours at a time. I would see Jason and Jonathan once a week also. I lived for their visits. Something would die inside each time I saw them pull away. I wanted so badly to go home with my family, but I knew I couldn't yet. I had a long way to go in order to be independent in my care.

In January, my father and little brother flew from the East Coast to see me. It was great to see them, but my father had a hard time dealing with my injury. Every time I looked at him, I saw a look of pity in his eyes. I knew it was going to require time to heal the hurt he was feeling for one of his sons. I was holding up really well, knowing that if I could show him I was OK, he would feel better. But one day, something happened to trigger a memory which caused me great pain. One day while in physical therapy, trying to scoot across a mat, I glanced over at Dad who was watching with the most painful look on his face. He sensed my frustration at having a problem trying to perform a task that a two-year-old could do better. A tear ran down his cheek. I'm sure that he was remembering the days that I was on the track team and had outrun everyone at a school of over 2,000 students. Suddenly, my thoughts went back twelve years, to an event that took place between my father and me when I was fifteen.

"Dad, I'm going to beat you this time," I said with excitement."

"We'll see, Son, but don't count me out quite yet. I've still got some kick left."

We walked up to the end of the road that ran in front of our house. Turning around and facing back in the direction that we had come from, we both knew the moment had come. Stretching before us was a one-hundred-yard long marked track, the end being our driveway.

"Dad, when this is over you are going to be eating my dust," I said with a look of boyish excitement on my face.

"Yeah, OK, Champ, let's see who is going to be eating whose dust. You have never beaten me yet. I know the day is coming, but not today," he said, chuckling.

We prepped for the race by leaning on our leading foot and facing the makeshift track in front of us.

"Dad, you say go. I don't want you to have any excuses when this is over."

"OK, Son. On your mark, get set . . ."

It seemed like an eternity waiting for him to say go. My dad was in great shape for a forty-year-old. He could outrun anyone I knew, but I was ready for him. Every muscle in my body was ready. My adrenalin raced, my young heart pumped blood to my pulsating muscles. I knew without a doubt that this was the day. "GO!"

We both shot out of our still positions like bullets out of a gun. We were both dead even after several yards. I ran like the wind with every muscle giving me 100-percent efficiency. At fifty yards we were still dead even. I had never been able to stay with him this long before. After seventy-five yards we were still even but I sensed that he was tiring. I knew he wasn't a quitter, I was going to have to outwork him. My body gave me an additional surge of energy and I somehow started pulling away. As we crossed the finish line I was ahead by a full stride.

"I did it," I yelled at the top of my lungs. I fought to regain my breath as we both slowed down. I glanced back to Dad only to see a strange look on his face.

"What's wrong, Dad?" I asked as we stopped running and I walked back to him.

"Son, the only way that you will understand how I feel right now is to go through it yourself," he said trying to catch his breath. "Two things are going through my mind. I am so proud of you. I have always told you that the day that you could outrun me you would be a man. Of course I was joking but as I look at you, you are a man. I know you have worked very hard for this moment. The other thing that I am thinking is that I am growing old. That's something that you won't experience for awhile but I know that someday your son will do it too. You'll see. It will be one of the proudest and saddest days of your life." He paused for a moment still trying to catch his breath. "But I can still out-arm-wrestle you," he said hitting me on the shoulder laughing. We walked back to the house slowly and I thought about what he had told me.

The memory faded. I was still staring at Dad as my thoughts came back to the present. Sitting right next to Dad was my son. Suddenly I realized, for the first time, that I would never have the same experience with my own son. I would never race him, chase him, or even walk with him. The thought of this tremendous loss hit me. Now the tears flowed down my cheeks. I lay down on the mat, hoping that if I didn't look at them anymore, I could ignore the feelings that were racing through my mind. It didn't work. I found myself crying out loud. I was embarrassed to be crying in front of my Father and all of the other patients, but I couldn't stop. Sue who was sitting beside me, seeing my predicament, walked over and asked my family to leave. I think she knew what was going through my mind. After they left, I was able to control myself. After a few moments, I got back up on my rear and started working my way down the mat again. Beth, who had witnessed the entire episode, walked over and sat down beside me.

"I knew that you were just hiding your feelings all of this time. From now on, I want you to stop acting so happy and like everything is OK, when everyone knows it's not. I knew all along that you were having problems," she said with a look of satisfaction on her face. She got up and walked off to help someone else.

My sadness was now turning to anger. It was as if she were just hovering around me, waiting to watch me fall. But I didn't say anything. I had enough problems without trying to argue with her. I knew if I argued with her, it would only serve to prove her point. I prayed about my attitude and soon I was over it. After finishing my therapy, I went out to talk with my family. I tried to explain to Dad what had happened but it was difficult to tell him how I felt without having him worry about me. I just told him that I was having a bad day and we both dropped it. The rest of Dad's and my brother's stay was fairly uneventful. We had a good time talking even though reminiscing was painful. It took several months before I could think about the past without being sad, but eventually with prayer, I would learn to cope with that aspect of my injury.

One of the most enjoyable times at Rancho was during the evenings. Dinner was served at around five o'clock, and I always enjoyed helping pass out the trays for those who couldn't help themselves. I was only too happy to use my strong arms to help those who could no longer use theirs. Most of us gathered in a large room to eat together. There we would talk about how our therapy was going, how we were injured, and how we felt about what was going on around us. After dinner came cruise time. Electric and manual wheelchairs would fill the halls to race, pop wheelies and generally cause the nurses to develop acute ulcers. We were never disruptive, but it was during this time that we would blow off the steam that built up on a daily basis. I learned and taught others that they had to have an escape valve, or this horror that we were all feeling would eventually destroy us. But I always did this in fun or constructive ways. Sleeping was one of the most difficult chores we had to accomplish. First of all, trying to sleep in a body jacket was hot and uncomfortable. We were also turned like a beef on a rotisserie every three hours, while we slept. The reason for this is that by switching positions the likelihood of getting decubitus (bedsores) was lessened. Each nurse was a successful graduate of the "One Hundred Unique Ways to Interrupt Sleep" course. They would come in, turn on the lights, and tell the latest in the new line of side-splitting jokes as they turned us over. Most of the time I was able to sleep through their rendition of "The Johnny Carson Show," but one night they were so loud that one of the other men spoke up. He asked them to take their jokes out into the hall, he was trying to sleep. The nurses reported to the head nurse that he was a disruptive patient. He was chastised for complaining and not them for their noise. Night was just something I eventually was able to sleep through. Some of the less fortunate light sleepers never grew accustomed to the noise and found themselves sleeping through therapy, for which they were penalized.

One day a psychologist came to see me. She said it was routine for her to visit with all of the patients to ascertain their current mental state. We talked for awhile about my physical condition and all of its ramifications.

I could tell that she was feeling me out as we spoke. She was an expert at talking, listening, and guiding the conversation so as to pick up on any psychological problems that might be occurring. I'm sure she got plenty of practice at a place like Rancho with so many severely injured people. After we were deeply involved in conversation and she felt I was comfortable in talking with her, she led into what she really wanted to know.

"How do you feel about yourself?" she asked with a pleasant smile on her face.

"I suppose you mean post injury."

"Not necessarily, but that's fine."

"Eight years ago I gave my heart and life to Jesus Christ. It was then that I started to like myself as I was. I guess that I am now coming to the place of getting to like myself again. I am not bitter at all. That left soon after the accident, but I am certainly not the same anymore. I am severely handicapped, and I'm still not sure of what all I'm going to be able to do."

I guess I passed her test. Before she left, she asked me if I would talk to some of the patients who were really down on themselves. In the months to come, that's just what I did. This turned out to be the best way to help myself too. It seemed that the more I helped other people, the better I felt about myself. As a matter of fact, in a later interview, she said that normally an attitude like mine was something that took years to develop and some never could. I told her I attributed the difference to Christ. I don't know if she agreed with my beliefs but she couldn't argue with the results.

As with most nurses and therapist students, the day for Sue to move on to her next assignment finally came. We said good-bye and hugged. I was going to miss her positive way of encouragement.

With little more than five weeks to go, I thought it was time that I approach Beth about the prospect of walking again. She replied, "No!"

10
The Battle of the Braces

"What do you mean, no?" I asked with unbelief.

"I mean," said Beth, "that your injury is so severe that you will *never* use your legs functionally again for walking. You are so big that your arms could not possibly support your weight for any duration. As I said when we first spoke about it, you will not be able to walk unless you have some leg movement. I have been through this so many times before with other patients. I know you want to walk, but that is simply not possible. You are just in for a big letdown. I know I would be wasting my time on a useless project when so many other people just need my time for basic skills. I know that you are so excited about walking that you can't see the forest for the trees. I have much more experience in this area than you. I am not going to go through the time and expense to do something that I know is useless. This is my final decision."

"I don't mean to argue, Beth, but if I don't try, I will never know what might have been. Just being able to stand up using braces would be good psychologically. The exercise will do me good. The biggest reason I've got to try is that I've promised my Sunday School class that I'm going to walk in some day. I have to try."

"The answer is still *no!* I am your physical therapist, and I know that we would just be wasting time. You must have some leg movement." She turned and walked away, taking my hope of ever walking again with her. She was standing between me and a dream, and I wasn't sure what to do.

I talked with Don (the resident priest) about my problem, and he suggested that we talk to the head of the hospital. Don was surprised that she wasn't even going to let me try. I refrained from this action because I wanted to try to get along with Beth, but I wasn't getting too far with that idea either. I finally resolved to talk with Beth's supervisor. I made an appointment with her and I told her what was on my mind. She acted somewhat surprised that Beth was not interested in letting me try.

"Beth is one of the best therapists I have. I will have a talk with her about this. This doesn't sound like her at all. I'm sure that you have misunderstood her in some way. I will see that Beth gives you an outline of all the requirements of walking using long leg braces and crutches. If you can meet them within the specified time, I guarantee you that you will get the opportunity to try to walk."

I was so excited about the prospect of getting an opportunity for ambulation trials, that I hugged her and made tracks for the obstacle course. I pushed my chair faster and farther than I had ever gone. My heart raced for the rest of the day. The evening passed incredibly slowly. That night I called Wanice, a few of my friends, and my parents with the good news. On the following day, I showed up at physical therapy early and rolled over to the parallel bars where ambulation trials were held. Beth walked by and gave me a look fit to kill and handed me a list of all the physical requirements that preempted walking.

"This is a big waste of time, but here is the list," she said as she walked past me in an effort to avoid confrontation.

"Beth, I promise that I'll work hard, and whatever is on this list, I'll give it my best shot."

"Rob, when are you going to get it through that thick skull of yours, that you are not going to be able to walk?" She looked down at the other end of the parallel bars and pointed to a young man with the same level of injury as mine. He was trying to stand up in the bars and faltering. His arms could not fully support his weight when he tried to take a step. He fell forward barely catching himself.

"Rob, look down there at Mike. He is younger and much lighter. He has a far better chance of walking than you do. His spinal chord was not severed like yours, either. You are just going to have to come down out of that cloud of yours and see reality. You went over my head to get this little list of yours, so here it is. Maybe after you see it you will learn to listen to my many years of experience." She turned and walked off in a rush. I couldn't believe how cold she was being. Why couldn't she encourage me in my efforts and let the results speak for themselves? But I was not going to let her attitude deter me from my goals. Here it was. It was all up to me now.

I looked at the list. It was staggering! The list was filled with requirements that ranged from strength, endurance, increased range of motion on my legs and much more. That night I lay in bed reading the list. I was overwhelmed at the task ahead. In order to meet all of the requirements,

I would have to be able to stretch both of my legs to reach a ninety-degree angle while lying on my back. I would have to meet a rigorous cardiovascular and oxygen test which entailed pushing bike pedals with my hands as long as I could. I would also have to meet a minimum time on the endurance track, keeping my heart rate down to a tolerable level. In addition, there were many other agility exercises. I would have to be able to do fifty parallel-bar dips without stopping, stand up for one hour at a standing table, which required unusual strength, be able to balance myself in the parallel bars using braces, and walk (swinging my legs) not less than two times the length of the bars. After reading the list I was almost numb at the thought of this awesome task. I was glad that at last I was going to be given a shot, but I was scared that I might not be able to do it. I recalled Beth's words to me.

"I am your physical therapist and I know that we would just be wasting my time. You must have some leg movement in order to walk."

I thought about the helplessness of my situation. I wanted to walk. Yet realistically I knew it was impossible without leg movement. I thought about how much easier it would be just to forget the whole thing. But I couldn't. I felt as if I would be causing a dream to perish—a dream that I believed in with all my being.

Besides, how could I glorify God if I felt He wanted me to walk again and I didn't try? It was going to take a miracle. I believed in miracles, but this was asking the impossible. *Or was it,* I thought. *God is in the business of doing the impossible. I've seen miracles before, so why not this?* I decided to turn it over to God.

"Dear Heavenly Father, I am asking You for a miracle. I want to walk back into Sunday School someday. I think it would be a faith builder for me and others who know me. I promise to accomplish everything on this list that I have the power to accomplish. I pray that You will accomplish the items on the list that I have no control over—chiefly leg movement. I promise to give You all the praise and glory. Amen."

Now that it was in His hands, I tried not to worry about it anymore. I would do everything I could do and depend on Him to do the rest. On the following morning, I started working even harder than I had before. My hamstrings were currently being stretched to an excruciating eighty degrees. I asked one of the therapists to stretch my legs at least two degrees further each day, so that five days later both of my legs would be at the required ninety degrees. With the aid of this therapist, and with the hope of walking again, I made it in four days.

In my weight-lifting class, I worked like a horse. I told the weight-lifting director about my goals.

"Bill, I want to try to walk again, and Beth tells me I need to be stronger. What is the current record for a combined pull using both of the pulley systems?"

"The standing record is 285 pounds set a few years ago by a former weight lifter."

"What is the maximum lift that you feel would be safe for me to attain?"

"The maximum weight that we are allowed to put on the weight system is 300 pounds, 150 pounds for each of the two exercises. That is a great deal of weight to pull in your position and with your level of injury."

"That is my goal then—300 pounds? I'll do it, too."

I began with 100 pounds, and increased this by five pounds each day. Two weeks later in a routine weight class, Bill set up the first pulley system for 150 pounds. The other patients were looking on in disbelief, but I believed I could do it. He tightened the belt which held me in my chair. This much weight could lift me right out of my chair. I took a few deep breaths, looked at Bill, and said "Here goes!" The bar was immediately over my head. The bar was attached to a cable which fed through a pulley system to weights that were placed behind me. I had to pull the bar down, lifting the weights off the ground. He positioned himself next to me to help in case I got in trouble. I started pulling slowly, I didn't want to just yank it. I wanted to be sure it was muscle that pulled the weight and not momentum.

At first the weights didn't move. I pulled harder. Slowly they began lifting off the ground. I continued to pull down even though my back was beginning to hurt. I was not going to stop. I pulled the bar down below my chin, even with my chest. I had done it! The patients cheered.

"Bill, set me up on the second event," I said with confidence. He moved the bars around while I waited, with my heart pumping and adrenalin filling my veins, Bill set up the second and more difficult lift.

"OK, it's all up to you," Bill said with a supportive voice. I placed my hands on the bar that was now chest high. I now had to put my hands on the bar and push it down to my lap. This exercise used triceps almost exclusively. I began driving the bar down. This time the weights moved even easier than before. Another round of applause went up around me. I glanced over and saw Beth watching me from a window. She walked away when she saw me looking. She never said anything to me about the lift. At my last check, the record still stands today.

I set a goal of sixty parallel-bar dips instead of the required fifty. I made it in less than three weeks. I met the requirements on the endurance track with several seconds to spare. My heart rate continued to lower with each passing day.

Then came the big day for the bicycle test. I was ready. A respirator was placed in my mouth that attached to a machine that measured the oxygen and carbon monoxide ratios in my respiration. I began turning the pedals slowly. The resistance was low to begin with. I turned the pedals on and on. My heart pumped, my lungs felt like bursting and my arms screamed with pain, but I kept turning. I wasn't going to quit until I could no longer move my arms. The doctor turned the level of difficulty up with each passing minute making the pedals harder to turn, but I kept going. After several minutes of torture my arms quit turning. I fell back into my chair completely exhausted. I stunned the therapist with one of the best Oxygen to Monoxide, and heart rates ever for my injury level on the bicycle test. One by one, I whittled away at the requirements on my list. Each morning I would try to lift my legs, hoping that the day had come for God to perform the miracle, but each time, I rolled away disappointed. The standing table was next. I would stand at the table for increasingly longer times until at last I could stand for one hour, using straps to hold the bulk of my weight. Soon I could actually stand at the table without straps for over fifteen minutes.

Next came walking in the parallel bars using braces. Beth fit me with two temporary long leg braces that reached from my upper thighs to shoes that were attached to the braces. They locked at the knee and were strapped on with straps and buckles. They were very heavy and cumbersome. Beth's goal for me was to walk to the end and back two times. I did it twenty times. I finally quit because the time was up, not because I was tired. Finally everything on the list was complete with the exception of leg movement and walking using braces and crutches outside of the parallel bars a few days later.

On the morning of March 24th, with about three weeks to go before dismissal, a strange thing happened. I was finished dressing and was just waiting for some assistance to put on my shoes. I called one of the nurses over to help me. She put my right shoe on and was reaching for my left foot, when I instinctively tried to raise my leg so that she could put my left shoe on. My leg raised up off of the bed about an inch and then

crashed back down. She looked at me and I looked at her. I thought she
had done it and she thought I had done it.

"Do that again!" she half screamed with a wild look in her eyes.

"Do *what* again? *You* did it, didn't you?"

"No, I didn't touch you!" she cried. "Do it again!"

"I'll try," I said with amazement in my voice.

This time I lifted it up about four inches before it slowly descended to
the bed.

"Don't go away," she said running out into the hall like a wild woman.
She returned with a small army of nurses, therapists, aides, and doctors.

"I understand you just did something out of the ordinary," my doctor
said with a skeptical look on his face.

"Just watch this," I said putting every bit of energy into my numb leg.
This time it rose more than a foot above the bed and I held it for about
three seconds before it fell back to the bed. My roommates by this time
were looking through the crowd that surrounded my bed. Everyone in
the room was filled with amazement. Some of them shook their heads in
disbelief. Others cheered. After my doctor had entered a few notes in his
medical records, the bulk of them left. What ensued was an argument as
to my classification. Beth told the doctor that my spinal cord was still
completely severed in her book. The doctor argued that if it was, I would
not be able to move my leg at all. I believe that Beth disliked me so much
that she did not want anyone to be encouraged (especially me) so that I
would not attempt to walk. Somehow she equated my walking with her
losing credibility because she would be proved wrong. I was amazed at
how far she was willing to go in order to be proven correct.

Some of my roommates were encouraged and thought if they worked
harder, anything was possible. I believed that to be true, but I explained
that I attributed the miracle to prayer first and hard work second. All of
the hard work in the world can not regenerate nerves. My leg movement
made believers out of several of them.

Two days later came the big day. I was to walk outside of the parallel
bars for the first time. Beth became increasingly short tempered with me.
Now nothing I did pleased her. With all of the mental strain I was under
just due to the ordeal that was about to take place, I was very near the
breaking point, and she knew it. Little did I know that she had found a
way to pull the rug out from under me. A few days earlier the driving
instructor had made an appointment for me on the same day and the
same hour as my first walk. A day before the walk took place, I called

him and asked for a different appointment time. He agreed and was very excited about my walking plans. I looked for Beth to tell her that in case she knew about the driving appointment that there was no conflict. I even told her assistant about the change in appointment times, and that I could walk at the prearranged time. At the appointed time I went into the physical therapy room and began putting on my own braces, which I had been doing for over a week.

I began the long tedious task of putting my braces on. This took about a half an hour of frustration and hard work. With little movement in the left leg and no movement in my right leg, it was a nearly impossible task. But I finally finished and stood up between the parallel bars to stretch out my back and work on my balance. I was going to need more balance using two crutches than the stable parallel bars I had grown accustomed to. During the entire time I had been putting on my braces I noticed a curious thing. Beth walked through the room to her office several times and back out to the wards. Each time she would glance over at me with a small smile on her face. In the meantime, another physical therapist walked over and started talking with me.

"Rob, I am so proud of you. You have really fought against the odds. I've watched your struggle to walk again and I respect you for it. I wish I had a few patients like you. I would even settle for one."

"Thank you. I appreciate your encouragement. I'm kind of nervous about this. I'm sure that walking with crutches is going to be tough. I am going to have to pick up my body weight and swing my legs forward and keep my balance while my legs are in the air. Another problem is that because I can't feel, I never know where my legs are. I have to look down at them with each step. I've come a long way, though, and I'm not going to let my fears stop me. I'm going to make it.

"I bet you will at that," she said with a smile on her face. We talked for a few moments and she tried to give me a few pointers which might make my walk easier. While we were talking, Beth walked up with a bitter look on her face.

"Are you ready, Beth? I feel like I could jog a mile," I said with a smile from ear to ear. "No, I have cancelled your walk. You are scheduled for a driving lesson."

The smile that I had plastered on my face slowly disappeared. I felt as if she had stabbed me and was turning the knife. *When was this one-sided rivalry going to end?* I turned and faced the wall so that she would not see the disappointment on my face. I figured it would give her satisfaction.

When I turned back around the bitter look that was previously on her face was replaced with a smile. I couldn't believe it.

"I wrote you a note and put it on my desk. I even told your assistant about the change in schedules."

"I didn't hear or see anything of the sort," she said walking away.

"Well, now you know. Why can't we do it now?"

"Because I have already scheduled other things to do right this minute. Besides the other two people who were to help are busy with other projects."

"If this is true, why didn't you tell me before while I was struggling to put my braces on?"

"All that I am concerned with is that you co-ordinate your schedule with me first. The next time make sure that you don't schedule two things at once."

I could have argued that I had tried in two ways to co-ordinate my schedule with her but I knew it was no use. Again I looked away from her. She had won. She was the therapist. I was the patient. She was in control. A big tear rolled down my cheek.

"Do you understand me?"

I felt as if I were crawling when I turned around and said, "Yes, I understand."

She walked away. The therapist that I had been talking to turned back to me with a look of surprise on her face.

"What was that all about? I can't believe that she talks to you that way. Why is she so down on you?"

"I wish I knew. I'm just trying to walk. I've got enough problems without having to fight her every step of the way."

The more I thought about it the madder I got. I'm through crawling. I ripped my braces from my legs and threw them down. I rolled out to an outside garden and sat there to cool off. One of the other therapists told me that no sooner than I had left, Beth ran to Mary her supervisor and told her that I had gotten mad and left. A few minutes later Beth and her supervisor walked by with Beth talking a mile a minute. In about twenty minutes the supervisor returned to hear my side.

"I just want to walk and Beth seems to want to stop me."

"Beth told me that you are one of her most difficult patients, and that you argue with her about everything. She also said that you were . . ."

"Look, I don't care what she has told you. Just ask around. Ask the other nurses and therapists, they will tell you who is telling the truth.

They have seen firsthand how she treats me. The only thing I want to do is walk. I don't know what Beth's problem with me is, but if she won't let me try to walk, I want a different therapist."

"No, I want you to work with her. Now go in and put your braces on and we'll go for that walk. I'll come with you and make sure that you get to walk right now. If you can do it, we'll continue ambulation trials. If not, the walking is over and I don't want to hear another word from either one of you about it."

I went into the therapy room, put my braces on for the second time, and waited for Beth. She walked past me without saying a word and walked out into the hall where we were going to walk. Mary walked over with a smile on her face and said, "Let's do it."

We all went into the hall. George, the largest male therapist, was there to help in case I began to fall. I was still uneasy because I probably out-weighed him too, but I was glad he was there just in case. Mary explained how I was to use the crutches to push off with and then, by moving them to the front quickly, I could stop the forward movement before falling forward. She also explained that because I could not functionally move my legs, I would use gravity to move them forward. In other words, by putting the crutches in front of me, at the approximate width of my shoulders, I would hop up to them using them for support and balance. This gate was called a "swing-to," because I was swinging my legs for-ward to meet the crutches.

"Are you ready, Rob?" Mary asked, still smiling.

"Yes, I'm a little scared, but I've come too far to turn back now."

"Good! You may get up whenever you like then. I have all the confi-dence in the world that you will do fine."

This was it! For three months I had worked for and anticipated this moment. I was trying to concentrate solely on this one important event, but it was difficult with Beth standing right beside me with her usual bitter look. For once, I wished that she could have been the one who was encouraging me. I wished that she were sharing in my excitement. But I tried not to dwell on the past and tried concentrating on the event that was before me.

"Here goes," I said, pushing on my crutches. Everyone moved into position in order to support me. Because I wasn't sure how hard to push, I had underestimated my weight and did not fully stand up. I crashed back down to the waiting wheelchair. The second time, putting more arm strength into it, I flew up to the standing position and was falling over forward when I caught myself with my crutches.

"I'm up," I cried, not believing I was actually standing. "Very good, but let's try standing up a few more times so that you get the hang of it," Mary said encouragingly.

"Anything you say. This is a great feeling," I said, beaming. I carefully sat down, following Mary's instruction about how far to be away from the chair. With two straight leg braces, once I started down, I was going and I couldn't change directions or distances relative to the chair. After several attempts at standing, Mary said the words I had been waiting to hear for months. "Let's go for a walk!"

"I'm ready," I said getting in position to take my very first step as a paraplegic. I planted my crutches up ahead and got ready for the hop. I wasn't sure how hard to push so I pushed down on my arms and tried to hop. My body swung forward on my arms and I almost fell forward, but I caught myself. I had forgotten that I did not have any rear muscles with which to keep myself from falling forward. Trying to compensate for this inequity, I learned that I must always keep the crutches well out in front of me. The effort was enormous and I was glad that I had worked as hard as I had. I took another eleven steps before I was totally exhausted. I sat back down in my chair and rested.

"That was very good for your first attempt. I think we should go ahead with ambulation trials, Rob. Many people cannot even take one step their first time outside of the parallel bars. Beth, you can handle it from here," Mary said over her shoulder as she walked off. Without a word to me she took my braces and we were through for the day. As she was about to walk off I said, "Beth, you were right. It was very difficult, but I'm glad I tried or I might never have known what might have been. Besides now I know what I'm up against. Thanks for your help."

"Uh-huh," she said as she walked off.

During the last two weeks of my stay at Rancho, I walked in the parallel bars several hours each day and took at least one walk a day putside the bars. Beth worked with me on improving my stance and gait, also on falling and standing back up. I was never completely successful at it because I was so afraid of falling. Beth and I got along a little better during the last two weeks. I was relieved. My longest walk while at Rancho was about 100 feet.

11
Going Home

Part of the rehabilitation at Rancho was going home for two weekends. The theory behind these two short visits was to introduce me to my home environment in small doses. Patients who had completed the program, and then had gone home, were totally overwhelmed with the new challenges. By going home during the therapy process, the staff was ready to help cope with specific problems that were encountered upon return to rehab.

My first trip home was in early April. I discovered something about my new life-style. As long as I stayed at the hospital I was normal, one of the many in a wheelchair. As a matter of fact, if anything, I was one of the lucky ones. I had two strong arms, I had broken all the weight-lifting records, and I was respected for who I was. But the moment I left Rancho, I was a severely handicapped person. I was the weak and frail one in comparison to everyone else. Suddenly I felt very peculiar and unprotected.

That night, I was greeted by most of our church friends at a dinner being held in the church parlor. On the following morning I called my boss. He was very awkward sounding on the phone and wasn't sure what to say. He had no way of knowing if I were bitter toward him and the company. I'm sure that it also bothered his conscience that he had only come to see me two times, neither of which I was conscious enough to remember. He joked on the phone about when I would be coming back to work, but we both knew he was just searching for something to say.

During the conversation he said, "I'm glad you called. Why don't you and Wanice come over and eat dinner with Mary and me tomorrow? We have much to discuss."

"Great, I'm looking forward to talk with you also. We'll see you after church tomorrow," I returned.

"See you tomorrow," he said trying to sound enthusiastic.

After we hung up, I thought about Jim's position. I didn't envy him. He was going to have to tell me that I no longer had a job with Pengo. I was sure that he was feeling very awkward, not knowing how to say it. I was going to make it as easy on him as I could. On the following morning Wanice, Jason, Jonathan, and I went to church for the first time since my accident. We had a great time. I told my Sunday School class about my walking. Everyone was moved. I said a few words during the worship hour to the congregation. It was hard to demonstrate my praise to God about walking while sitting in a wheelchair, but I did anyway. It was then I decided that soon I would walk down the aisle one Sunday morning, demonstrating God's power over impossible situations.

After church Wanice and I went to Jim and Mary's house. Jim was charcoaling some steaks on the grill so I rolled through the house to the backyard patio with him while Mary and Wanice remained in the house preparing the rest of the meal. Jim brought me up to date on the business. We talked and laughed about some of the experiences that we had shared. I glanced in through the window at the girls and they were very serious. Wanice told me later that Mary was so upset about the accident that she could barely speak. She told Wanice how many times that she and Jim had started to come and see me, but that Jim was just too upset to come. They had cried many hours together. Mary said that Jim just kept repeating "Why Rob? Of all the people I know, why did it have to happen to Rob? He is a good and godly man. I don't understand it."

Meanwhile, out in the backyard, Jim and I had run out of subjects to talk about. We both knew what I was really there to discuss. I broke the silence.

"Jim, it's evident to both of us that I can no longer perform the same duties I used to. The oil field is no place for a paraplegic. So I guess the question is whether you can use an extra salesman or an office person in some sort of administrative capacity."

He thought long and hard. I was aware this was not a new question for him. I'm sure he had considered this possibility before. He was not thinking of what to say, but how to say it. After a few seconds, he lowered his eyes to the ground.

"Rob, I wish I could tell you that we were busy enough to justify you as a salesman, but we're not. So I don't believe we can use your services any longer. However, I did talk to your old boss, Jim Robertson. He said that he might be able to use you at the corporate office back in Fort Worth. I told them that if they did want you back there, we would pay for your move back."

Jim had such a painful look on his face that I changed the subject. Soon after we ate, Jim and Mary drove me back to the hospital. Sleeping that night was difficult, realizing I was out of a job, but I gave it to God in prayer and rolled over to sleep.

The following day was Monday, between a couple of my classes, I called Jim Robertson.

"Jim, this is Rob Bryant."

"Well, hello, Rob. How are you getting along?"

"Fine, Sir. I'm calling because I talked with Jim Clemans, and he told me you might want me to come back and work for you. Is that true?"

"Well, it was true. But right now we are in the middle of a large change in our corporate structure. We are under a hiring freeze. So the money that we had set aside for your return is no longer here. I will call you back in a week or so; I will know more about our stability then. It's been nice talking with you. Keep in touch."

"OK, Jim, I'll talk to you in a week."

We hung up, and I felt as if a part of me had been removed. My hope of continuing my employment with Pengo was becoming dimmer. How was I going to support my family now? I thought about poor Jonathan and the mess that he had been born into. I was willing to do anything in order to keep food on the table. With my paycheck cut off and our savings quickly being depleted, I was desperate. Once again I prayed about my situation and tried to forget about it for a week until I would call Jim Robertson back. This was a near impossible task. I tried to concentrate on my ambulation trials. I was thankful that Beth was trying to get along with me. With everything else on my mind, I didn't need any additional complications.

Slowly the week passed and Jim didn't call back. After ten days with no word, I called him.

"Jim, this is Rob."

"Hello, Rob. I'm glad you've called. I have talked with everyone. The president told me to tell you to come on back home and that your old job would be waiting for you. I'm glad too, we can sure use your talents back here. Since you left, all of the technical writing has fallen behind. I'll see you when you get back. Good-bye."

"Good-bye, Jim."

I almost jumped out of my chair when we hung up. I yelled, "Thank You, Jesus!" Everyone in the room turned around and I told anyone who would listen about what God had done for me. I called Jim Hurst and Steve Burdette, two friends from home, and asked them if they would find a rental house for me and my family. Just four days later, they called back and said they had found the perfect house. I was reminded how rich in friends I was. I wired the money right away.

With little more than a week to go, I worked hard on my ambulation and transfers. The fear that I had experienced during the weekend began to plague me. The time was near for me to leave the confines of the hospital. Soon my protection from the world would come to an end. As soon as I rolled out of those protective doors, I was a cripple to be pitied.

Before I could prepare for it, the big day came. April 12, 1983, was my Independence Day. Fear of the unknown crept up on me, but I fought back against it. I was going to take charge of the situation and not let it dictate my feelings to me. I took one last walk with Beth. After it was over I thanked her for her help and I gave her a hug. It was hard on both of us. I think her conscience was bothering her about how she had treated me, yet at the same time she could never voice it. We were both close to tears during the bittersweet moment. I said good-bye, and I rolled away from her for the last time. I believe we were both relieved that the time had come. It was time to get on with my life and I did not want to look back.

Wanice arrived at ten to pack my bags. I said good-bye to the nurses for the last time. I made a special trip back to my room to say good-bye to Grant and Mike. It was hard leaving the people I had shared such hard times and good times with. A few minutes later, I was in the car leaving Rancho. Suddenly my fears gave way to a stronger emotion—freedom! I could sleep with my wife, play with the kids, and conquer fresh goals in my new life-style. Little did I know that in less than a year I would return and shock everyone with a surprise.

The whole family was excited to see Daddy home again. I played with Jason and Jonathan nonstop for two days. I put Jason on my lap and we went down to a nearby park. I felt so confined, but I decided that my kids were not going to suffer any more than they already had. I tried to do everything I used to do with Jason before my accident. It was hard explaining to Jason that I couldn't do everything other Dads could do, but he seemed to understand and was very patient when I had difficulty doing ordinary tasks. Often I would see Jason standing nearby studying me as if I were a stranger. His favorite statement to me was, "One of these days you'll feel better and walk again." I hated to tell him that unless

God miraculously healed me, I would never walk again. Every night Jason prayed that his Daddy would someday walk again. Believe me, I prayed along.

Wanice acted the same towards me as before the accident. The only difference being that she cried and laughed very easily. For instance, on my first night home, I needed a bath. The bathroom was upstairs, so we contemplated several options when we finally decided that the only way was to spray me with a hose out on the porch. It was surrounded by a wall, but it was not very high. I took my clothes off and went out to the porch. I transferred out of my chair onto the hard concrete. She sprayed me with the hose in the fifty-degree air. I began shivering. Upon looking around, I discovered that any one of ten neighbors could see us from the second floor of the next condominium. I was washing with soap when she began laughing. I began laughing also. We laughed until I finished. After going back into the house, Wanice began crying. When I asked her what was wrong, she wouldn't answer. I knew that she had probably cried each day that I was in the hospital. I was at awe at her faith in God and love toward me. She was truly a Proverbs 31 kind of woman. Her faith was increasing in strength weekly. I was amazed at how much she had grown in the Lord in my absence. She explained to me that while I was in the hospital, God had been her Protector, Husband, Companion, and Friend. He had taken my place during my absence. I felt that I had some pretty big shoes to fill now that I was back to be her husband.

Wanice and I began saying good-bye to our California friends. It seemed like all I had been doing for weeks was saying good-bye. "One of these days we'll never have to say good-bye again. We'll share paradise together. Not only that, but I'll walk again. Heck with walking, I'll fly," I told Tom, a friend of mine.

Never before had I longed to go to heaven quite so badly. Not that I wanted to die, but for the first time I wanted what heaven had to offer right now.

Our church friends loaded up our furniture on a truck and tied our car to the back. One of my work buddies drove the truck back to Fort Worth for us. During the last week, we stayed with Tom and Dorothy Pettigrew, some friends from church. They had had us over just two weeks before my accident for a Thanksgiving meal with their family. They knew that we didn't have any family in the area. They taught Wanice and me a lot about hospitality.

Then came the twenty-third of April, the day we would fly back to
Fort Worth. I called Jim Hurst and told him what time to pick us up at
the Dallas/Fort Worth Airport. He asked if we minded if a few friends
came to meet us. I said no.

The Petersons and Wilsons spent the day with us and then took us to
the Long Beach airport. With lumps in our throats, we went out to the
plane that would take us from our new friends back to our old friends. I
was met at the bottom of the stairs by two gorilla-looking baggage men
who helped me into a thin chair. I took one look at the tall stairs and
turned white, they took one look at me and turned blue. "We'll have you
in your chair in no time," one of them said. The other man whispered,
"You and who else?"

They literally carried me up the stairs and back to my seat. Gasping,
I'm sure they wondered if they had picked the right line of work. Or if I
planned on flying with them often—the wrong airline. The three-hour
flight seemed like six, but we finally landed. We waited for everyone else
to exit the aircraft. Two more unsuspecting baggage men helped me off
the plane to my waiting wheelchair in the extended walkway that
reached from the plane to the terminal. Considering it was 10:30 at night,
I figured that most of my friends would not come, having children of
school age. However, as I looked up the long hall, I could see many familiar yet curious faces peering around the corner at me. Since I left as
strong as a horse and was returning in a wheelchair, I knew my emotions
were going to be a problem. I stopped for a second to fight back the
feelings. Once under control, I continued. I asked Wanice to walk beside
me. I felt like a stranger even among my own friends. Would they still
treat me the same or would I see pity in their eyes? There was only one
way to find out. I pushed my way up the hall. One of the baggage men
wanted to help me but I had to do it myself. Wanice and I entered the
terminal at the same time. Suddenly a loud cheer broke the silence. Everyone ran over to us and I was hugged and kissed by over thirty people
almost simultaneously. All my fears were put to rest. They would have
been my friends no matter how I came back to them.

We all went like a mob to the baggage reception area to get my lug-
gage. By the time we got to our cars it was after 11:30 PM and everyone
started drifting home. I rode with my old buddy Jim Hurst who told me
all about the house we were renting. He asked me all about my ongoing
physical therapy. It was good to talk to my old friend. I was relieved that
our friendship just picked up where we had left off. I spent that night at

my in-laws' house. We talked into the early morning.

The following day, Wanice and I went over to our house. It was perfect. It had large rooms, a huge hall, and wide doors. A friend of ours had widened the bathroom door so that my wheelchair would pass through. Our Texas friends already had our furniture unloaded. They helped Wanice unpack all of the boxes. Wanice and I were glad to be home again, but we already missed our California friends.

The following week was spent arranging all of the furniture and kitchen so that I could reach everything and take care of the kids when Wanice was away. I also stopped by Pengo to talk with Jim Robertson about my start-up date. But most of my effort was focused toward the walk that I had worked toward for close to five months. My old friend Jim Hurst came to the house every night for a week in preparation for the big moment. I practiced standing up and hopping. I was frustrated that I could not even walk twenty feet or so without being totally exhausted, since I had not worked out or practiced walking since my discharge three weeks earlier. This was really depressing considering that I had to walk over 100 feet to walk the length of the hall at church.

I had come too far and worked too hard to give up. I just believed that God was going to answer my prayer and help me when I would stand up to walk that next Sunday. The days flew by and suddenly it was Sunday morning. My stomach was in knots. I knew that my class had been praying for me and shared my dream and that they were all gathered to see it happen. I was excited yet nervous. I rolled into the Love (Sunday School) Building as we called it, and went to the end of the hall. I turned around and looked down it. Suddenly I realized just how far 100 feet really was. I put all thoughts of failure out of my head. Jim walked up behind me and helped me put my braces on. Jim and I said a quick prayer for strength and a calm heart. I stood up and faced the classroom.

"Here it is. This is what I have believed in and prayed for ever since my accident," I told Jim quietly.

"If anyone can do it, you and God can," Jim said in return.

I fought the tears that were trying to force their way out. I was going to have to focus all of my energy into the next several minutes. I didn't want to waste any energy on my emotions. I looked at the path with victory in my eyes. I started hopping toward my class. A few friends quickly walked by me and entered my classroom. I couldn't understand why my friends had just walked away and left me in the hall. I figured that they would walk with me in a spirit of encouragement. Maybe they figured that this was an emotional moment for me and left me alone. The hall slowly emptied and it grew very quiet. I kept hopping. Ninety feet to go, eighty, seventy, then sixty. I stopped in utter exhaustion. Jim patiently waited with one hand on my shoulder and the other on my lower back for support. This allowed me to lean back enough to take some weight off of my arms.

"OK, let's finish the job," I whispered over my shoulder to Jim.

I started hopping again. Forty feet to go, thirty, twenty, ten. I turned at the door way and completed a few more hops to get through the door. Suddenly a loud roar of applause rang through the air. Everyone stood up and cheered. They had been inside the room praying for me. That's why they had walked away. I leaned up against the wall as they continued to cheer. The song leader led us all in a prayer thanking God for answering our prayers. I believe that everyone who was present that day walked away having a greater faith in the power of prayer.

That next week, I started work. Although I was doing the same job I had done just ten short months prior, it seemed like another lifetime. Everyone around me helped in any way they could. Within a couple of weeks I was back at it in full swing.

In May of 1983 my entire Sunday School class went on a rafting trip to the Guadalupe River in Central Texas. It was then I learned something that would change my life forever.

The first problem was getting into the raft. We couldn't figure out a way to get me down to the river that was lined with steep banks. After investigating the river for several hundred yards, one of my friends found a suitable place for me to meet the rafts. With much help, I made it down into the river and we pushed my wheelchair out to one of the rafts as it passed by. During the following six hours we had races, got out and swam, drifted peacefully, and just had fun. I surprised myself by having enough strength to swim upstream in wide areas, just by using my arms. But it wasn't until everyone stopped to play on a waterfall that I felt left out. Up until then we were all sitting down and paddling so we were all equal, but with everyone running around by the falls, I became handicapped again. I just sat there contemplating my dilemma and getting more depressed by the minute. Everyone had walked through the waist deep water to a small waterfall and were swimming underneath it.

Well, I can either sit here and feel sorry for myself and be consumed with self-pity, or try to do as much as I possibly can despite my handicap, I thought.

Taking a deep breath, I fell into the water backwards like a scuba diver and began to swim back to the surface and upstream. I re-submerged a few seconds later only to find that I was already five feet downstream from the raft. I fought against the current as hard as I could, but I was still losing ground. I was in trouble. Luckily for me, Jim Hurst saw me and dove into the river and was by my side in seconds. With him standing on the bottom and my swimming as hard as I could with my arms, we slowly made headway. Minutes later we had successfully made it to the base of the raft. Jim tried to push me back into it thinking that I had fallen out by accident.

"No, I want to go to the falls with the rest of you," I said.

Knowing he wasn't going to talk me out of it, we headed for the falls. Jim continued to swim against the current pulling me. I found that I could reach the bottom with my hands, so I grabbed rocks on the bottom and pulled myself along. Several minutes later, I was with everyone else under the falls. I turned to Jim, "A man can do anything with God's help, the will to do it, and enough friends."

We played for the next half hour under the falls. Later that day one of my friends recounted his view of what had happened and decided the following.

"You know, if you want to sit and feel sorry for yourself, people are willing to let you do that. They've got problems of their own. On the other hand, if you are in a tough situation and are fighting back, they are willing to help you. Seeing you face your problems, and conquering them, gives them hope that they can face and conquer theirs."

Jim Hurst and I began working out three times a week in my garage. I had gotten flabby since my dismissal from Rancho and I needed the extra power if I wanted to continue walking. Wanice bought us a bench press with leg lifts. Soon I was actually lifting two or three pounds with my legs on the leg lifts and benching over 200 pounds. Although my legs were small, my upper body began to look good. After lifting weights, I walked on our sidewalk. I began to extend my fifty feet hopping record to over 100 feet.

One day during our evening walk on the sidewalk Jim said:"Why don't you try moving your legs independently, more like a stride instead of a hop."

"Because I can't, that's why."

"Come on, try it. What's it going to hurt?"

Just to prove him wrong I stood up and tried to move my left foot forward. It went forward slowly and awkwardly, but it went. I tried moving my right leg forward, but it wouldn't move by command. I had an idea. I moved my left leg forward again and dragged my right leg up to meet it. It worked!

I repeated the stride several more steps. It wasn't pretty but it was faster and more energy efficient. This marked the first day since my accident that I really took a step, instead of hopping. I set a goal for myself to walk to the end of the block in one hour. Within a month I did it. My left leg began to get even stronger as I increased the demand on it.

In June of 1983, I went to the Dallas Rehabilitation Institute (DRI) for the first time. I would be an outpatient there for years to come. There I met Doctor Wharton and Patty Stancliff, my physical therapist. They would change my whole outlook on walking in the future. I couldn't believe it, but Patty actually encouraged me in everything I was attempting to accomplish. This was so foreign to me after having worked with Beth, that I was in shock. One of my goals was to walk up a flight of stairs in order to teach a Sunday School class in the youth division of our church. I shared this goal with Patty. After Patty examined my legs for a few minutes, she said, "I don't see why you couldn't use a short brace (from the knee down) on your left leg. It sure looks strong enough to me. You see, if we can get your left leg strong enough to bend and step up, you will be able to climb stairs. Let's give it a try." She fitted me with a temporary knee-to-ankle brace and I actually took a few steps with it. Patty had my old brace cut down to below the knee. And had me fitted for new light plastic ones as well. Soon with her help, I was walking even faster. Within two months of extensive therapy, prayer, and determination, I climbed the stairs to my very first Sunday School class. I've been teaching ever since.

One day while getting in my car to leave the hospital, requiring a transfer using massive movement and energy, I felt a pop in my back. I felt a sharp pain strike me squarely between my shoulder blades. I thought something had hit me in the back, but I couldn't see anything. I reached around to where I felt the pain and discovered an unusual bump on the left side of my back bone. Slowly the pain went away and I drove home. But this pain came and went and grew steadily worse.

Soon after, Larry Mullens, a close friend, gave me the money to buy a racing wheelchair. I bought a beauty, and was able to round out my workout program with a cardiovascular exercise. I would pump out ten to twelve miles at a time. It felt good to do an exercise that would actually make me breath hard. But on one occasion when out on a long run, the sharp pain returned, only this time much more severely. It took me over an hour to cover the short distance home, as moving my arms caused me such great pain. After arriving home Wanice and I drove straight to the hospital. Patty Stancliff met us at the door and I went straight to X-Ray. I hand carried the X-Rays to Dr. Wharton's office. He carefully examined them one by one, holding them up to the light, as Wanice and I held our breath. He shook his head and lowered the X-Rays away from the light.

"Rob, I've got some bad news for you. The pain you feel is caused by one of the steel rods that were placed in your back during surgery. It has completely popped out of place. This could be caused from any number of things, not wearing your body jacket long enough, too much activity, or a bad rod insertion. I notice also that the rods are very short for a person of your size and activity level. But for whatever reason, your rods will need to come out. I will replace them if your backbone has not fused properly. Inversely, if your backbone has fused, I will simply remove the rods and not replace them. I will get you a room at the hospital tonight and I will operate in the morning."

"How long do you think I will be in the hospital?" I asked, almost afraid to hear his answer.

"If I just remove the rods your entire stay will be about three weeks. If I replace them, you'll be with us for about six weeks!"

"Please, Dr. Wharton, don't replace them unless you absolutely have to. I'm so tired of being in hospitals."

"I know. Believe me, I don't do things unless I feel they are absolutely necessary."

The next morning my back was shaved and I was given a light anesthesia. Minutes later, I was taken to surgery and placed on a rotating table, which would be flipped over after I was under a much stronger anesthesia.

"Are you ready, Rob?" I heard off in the distance.

"Let's do it, but remember I don't want those rods replaced."

"I'll see what I can do," came Dr. Wharton's familiar voice.

"I'm going to start the anesthesia now. It takes effect very quickly. Just relax and breath normally. You should start to feel sleepy and . . ."

12
Count It All Blessing

The waves must have been twenty feet high. I was face up in a life preserver that was floating on the water, yet the waves were gentle and hypnotic. It didn't seem to matter that I was miles from anywhere. I was so relaxed I didn't have to move my arms to stay afloat. I felt like a cork just bobbing helplessly on each wave.

Slowly I became aware of a nagging pain in my back. At first the pain was very distant, but it was getting stronger by the minute. Soon it was a sharp pain. The waves seemed to be getting bigger and more violent. Now I was being tossed about. I clung to the life preserver causing even more pain in my back. I fought to keep my head above the water. Soon I was fighting to hold onto the preserver and the pain in my back was so severe that I was screaming out loud. It felt as if someone had stuck a knife in my back and was slowly turning the blade. My arms became tangled up in the preserver somehow and I could not move them. Soon I was fighting for each breath. Suddenly my surroundings were disappearing. Was I drowning? I fought all the harder.

"Rob," came a voice from the darkness with an echo.

"Lie still!" The voice sounded familiar somehow.

"Lie still? I'll drown," I replied to the voice from the darkness.

I became aware that my eyes were closed. Upon opening them, I was looking Wanice square between the eyes.

"Lie still, you'll hurt yourself. You're not suppose to move at all," she said, trying to sound convincing.

"How do you feel?" she asked with concern written on her face.

"My back is killing me. Please get me a painkiller right away." She disappeared into the hall quickly to get a nurse. While I was waiting I noticed a funny thing. The ceiling was moving. The ceiling was moving? That didn't make sense. No, my bed was slowly tilting to the side. Within seconds I was facing the wall. I was going to fall out. Suddenly I realized that my arms and legs were strapped down to the bed. I was going to fall and I couldn't do anything about it. But just as soon as I was going to call for help, it stopped tilting and headed back the other way. The bed continued until I had tilted 180 degrees and was facing the other wall. Then it stopped once again and I headed back in the opposite direction. This explained my dream about the waves and my arms being tied up in the life preserver. When I found myself staring back at the door, Wanice and a nurse reentered. The nurse gave me a shot in my arm and told me that I could have one every four hours. I didn't know how I was going to survive four hours between shots, but I shook my head to acknowledge her statement. The nurse left and I looked back at Wanice. I could tell by the look on her face what the doctor had done, but I asked anyway.

"What did Dr. Wharton do to my back?"

"He had to replace the rods in your back and re-fuse your backbone with a piece of your Iliac crest from your hip bone. He said you were going to have to wear a body jacket for SIX MONTHS," she said with a look of compassion.

"Six months? I can't believe it. What is this contraption I'm lying on anyway? I feel seasick on this wave machine."

"It's a rotary bed designed to move your body weight around and keep it off your back most of the time. You will be on it for over a week!" As uncomfortable as it was, it did work. The days continued to pass slowly and before I knew it, a week had passed. The pain lessened to a bearable amount. It really irritated me that I couldn't watch TV because half of the time I was facing the walls and I couldn't see the screen. I couldn't read a book because my arms were strapped down and I couldn't hold it. But I toughed it out. What choice did I have? My friends started coming by, but I wasn't very much company as it was so painful to talk. On the eighth day my body jacket was delivered and I was placed into a standard bed with the jacket that I would wear for the next six months. On the tenth day, I was moved to Dallas Rehabilitation Institute by ambulance for at least six weeks of therapy and recovery.

For the first couple of days, I had to remain in bed because of a nasty case of staph infection in my back. During the next week I began to learn how to live, dress, bathe, work, and play in a body jacket again. I had forgotten just how painful and confining it was. I couldn't reach anything or lean forward without the body jacket cutting into my legs. During the second week, I began walking and lifting weights again. I couldn't exercise very much at all without my back hurting or my getting my body jacket in the way.

Like most tragedies, the full impact didn't hit me for a while. One night with about twenty of my friends at my bedside, it finally caught up with me. I began to get angry that all of my friends were walking around my bed with strong legs. But what really caused the most pain was when they innocently started talking about playing tennis together later. Suddenly anger gave way to sorrow and I began to cry out loud. I was so embarrassed. Several of them just put their arms around me or held my hand while I wept. They felt as helpless as I did. Everyone grew quiet.

"I'm so tired of it," I sputtered. "I'm tired of the pain and handicaps. I want to be normal, and play a game of tennis with you guys. I want to be strong again."

Gene Eatherly, my former Sunday School teacher, cleared his throat to speak and everyone turned to him.

"Rob, words cannot express how you have touched my life. I see in you such strength and courage in order to face each day. When I get depressed with a little problem, I think of you and know I can make it through the day if you can. You have been a good friend through the years and have done so much for me and I feel helpless now when you need me. There is just one way I can help you and that is to pray. I am going to pray that God will bless your life and cause some good to come out of all of this. I am going to pray that God will put a miracle in your life that makes even unbelievers stand back. I believe God will answer my prayer and like Jim says, if anyone can do it, you and God can."

He bowed his head and began to pray the most beautiful uplifting prayer that I have ever heard. After he finished others began to pray. Over half an hour later, I was a different person. I finished with a prayer of my own. I'm glad that God was about to give me a king-sized piece of grace to swallow because the next six months were going to prove to be the most emotionally damaging days that I had encountered to date.

That night when Wanice came to see me, we talked about my walking goals.

"Wanice, right now I can walk the length of our block and back in one hour. What kind of a goal do you think I can set for next year?" I asked inquisitively.

"Let's see. One year from today would be around July Fourth. How about walking from Dallas to Fort Worth?" she joked. I knew she was kidding, but for some reason I didn't laugh. *Is a walk like that possible in one year for a man who can barely walk a block?* I wondered. I knew who could help me. Patty!

On the following day, I got up and dressed as quickly as a paraplegic can dress and ate some breakfast. At 8 AM, I met Patty as she walked into the therapy area.

"Patty, I think I've got an attainable goal for myself, and I want your reaction. Do you promise not to laugh?"

"Yes, what is it?"

"What would you say if I said I wanted to walk from Fort Worth to Dallas, one year from now?"

She looked as if she had been shocked out of her wits.

"Well, my initial response would be that it can't be done by a person with your injury level. I'm not saying you shouldn't try if you feel strongly about it, but I will say that it has never been done before," she said, and then paused to think.

"I think if you want to do it, you should try. My only word of caution is that you might further injure yourself in this attempt. I want you to weigh the potential cost against the potential gain of a project like this."

For the first time since the thought had originally entered my mind, I was really considering attempting it. I became obsessed with the idea of walking the twenty-four miles from Fort Worth to Dallas. I decided to pray about it for a month before making up my mind.

One week later, I went home and was back to work a few days after that. I had missed only three weeks of work. A representative from the Texas Rehabilitation Commission told me that as far as she knew that was a record for returning to work after major back surgery.

For the next three months, I was going to have a home nurse come by each night and help me dress, clean my incision as it was still painfully infected, help with baths and assist with my bowel and bladder programs. I didn't like my privacy being invaded, but I didn't have a choice in the matter. It was either this or stay in the hospital, so I decided to make the best of the situation. I loved being back at work. I took on new projects and was working even faster than before my second surgery. Although sitting in my chair for eight hours caused me great pain, I was thankful to have a job and tried to ignore it.

One day at work a strange thing happened. I was working at my desk when a scene flashed into my mind. I saw myself walking to Dallas and crossing a finish line. I saw television cameras, reporters, and a mob of people around. I saw ensuing TV interviews and newspaper articles. I even saw a book with my name on the cover. I was so excited about it I called Wanice and told her all about it. I could tell that she thought I had finally gone over the edge. But I knew without a shadow of a doubt that God was behind it and that He wanted me to walk from Fort Worth to Dallas. If I did do it, everyone including me knew for a paraplegic to walk that far, it was going to take a bonafide miracle. It was that day that I decided to do the Miracle Walk, and that is the title I gave it from the very beginning.

In the past, I had learned that when God has promised to do something, the devil fights back. I shouldn't have been surprised at what was about to happen, but I have to admit it did have that effect. Just days after I made public my intention to do the Miracle Walk, dark times set in. One day soon after, my boss walked past my desk and asked me to step into his office.

"Well, Rob, how are you feeling?"

"Pretty good, Jim. My back still hurts, but I'll make it."

"Good, because what I have to tell you is not going to be easy for either one of us. As you know, Pengo is still not out of the woods financially and I have the painful duty to cut costs at every opportunity. Of course one of those costs is labor. I am afraid that as valuable as you are to the company at this time, I am going to have to lay you off in the very near future. I am going to keep you on the payroll as long as possible, but I'm afraid that period may not be very long. As I look around the office, I believe that you are the hardest worker I have on my team. But I have little choice but to suggest that you start looking for employment elsewhere and I will keep you as long as I possibly can."

I rolled out of his office a broken man.

That night the attack would continue. My nurse came over to help me with my daily routine. She started the water running in the bath and helped me out of my clothes. I transferred from the bed to the wheelchair with her help and went into the bathroom. Again she helped me transfer from the wheelchair to a bath seat. I was looking forward to the day when I could take a bath without my body jacket on so I could really get clean. I just sat there thinking of my conversation with my boss when suddenly I realized that steam was rising out of the bath tub. Looking over, I noticed that the mirror was covered with steam. I looked down at the water that was streaming across my feet only to see red spots on the top part of my feet. I reached down to turn the cold water on some more. It wasn't on at all, she had turned the hot water on and had forgotten to turn on the cold. With no sensation from the waist down, I had no way of feeling if the water was hot or cold. I pulled my legs out with the use of my arms and looked down at my feet. They were severely blistered. I called for my nurse and she came in and readjusted the water as if that was going to fix everything. I was too depressed to argue with her so I finished my bath, after which she helped me dress. On the following morning my feet were so swollen and red that I couldn't even wear my shoes. I was almost glad I couldn't feel them. I left work early and went to DRI to get them looked at. I had second-degree burns all the way up to my ankles. They told me that I could not walk for at least two weeks. This nearly killed me but hard times were just beginning.

A few days later while at home, Jason walked up to me and told me he wished that I was like the dad in one of his books.

"What do you mean Jason? What book?"

"The Daddy Book!"

"Go get it and show me, Jason," I replied curiously.

He disappeared into his room and came back a few seconds later with *The Daddy Book.* I opened it and on the very first page it showed a dad carrying his son on his shoulders. On each page was a picture of a big strong daddy doing things with his son—like chasing and playing tag, climbing trees, riding a bike, and so on. As I looked at the pages and saw how badly Jason wanted me to be like the dad in the book, I couldn't stand it. But mostly what bothered me was the look I saw in his eye. It was disappointment. "Jason, I'm sorry I can't be like this dad, but I try very hard to do everything with you that I can. I want to do all the things in this book, but I can't. I hope you understand that. It's not that I don't want to play with you this way, but it's just not possible. Do you understand?"

"Yes, I understand, Dad, but I still cry for you and me because you can't walk." That was what made me break. He jumped up in my arms and we both cried together. What had happened between us was painful, but I was glad we had it out in the open and not just pretend that it didn't exist. I was proud that Jason had the courage to confront the situation and want to talk about it so openly with me. We both grew closer during those moments and I decided that I didn't ever want to see that look of disappointment in his eye. I was going to work very hard at being as normal as I could with both of my boys. They had suffered enough, I didn't want my handicap to stand in the way of their happiness or their respect for me.

If this weren't enough, I was attacked again. This time it was the *coup de grace*. I was out in my racing wheelchair getting some needed sunshine and exercise. I had just completed a ten-mile trip, and was feeling really good about it. With less than a mile to go, I was pumping my arms as hard as they would go. I felt like Rocky when he ran up the stairs after he had the best run of his life. I was coming up to an intersection where I saw a lady walking out to the curb to cut me off. I was making such good time I was thinking about going around her, but I heard a car about to pass from the rear, so I was forced into stopping at her feet. She looked down at me with an all-knowing face and asked me a straightforward question.

"Young Man, have you accepted the Lord Jesus Christ into your heart as your personal Savior?"

"Yes, I have," I said with a smile from ear to ear.

She slowly looked down at my chair and then back to my face. "I don't think so. If you were a Christian, you would have the faith to get up and walk. By His stripes you were healed. You are nothing but a bad witness if you say you are a Christian, yet sit in a wheelchair."

"Do you mean that every time you get sick that you have lost your salvation, were never saved, or just outside of God's will?" I asked her in total shock at her callousness.

"I just don't believe a Christian ever has to be ill or hurt, and that's biblical," she said with a defiant look in her eye.

I wasn't in the mood to argue with her so when the traffic was clear, I went around. She would not step aside and was yelling after me that I needed to repent of the sin that was keeping me in the chair and be saved. If I wasn't beaten before, I was then. I was a totally defeated person. I was about to be laid off, with burn scars on my feet stopping me from walking with braces. In addition, Jason was deeply hurt by my accident. After getting home, I lay down in my bed and tried to explain to Wanice what was wrong, but it was no use. Just one month after deciding to walk from Fort Worth to Dallas and give God all of the glory, I was beaten and tired and really didn't care if I lived or died. I went to work Monday through Friday, went to church on Sunday, and just sat around the rest of the time. I was able to fool most people around me into thinking that I was happy, but I knew better. I tried to write the book that I had seen in my mind, but it was no use. My hope was gone. The devil had won his fight to stop the "Miracle Walk."

13
"You Can Do It, Dad!"

"Really fill it up this time, Dad," Jason said with a look of excitement. I filled the rocket to the halfway mark and placed it onto the pump. Pumping the handle about ten times, I held the rocket out in front of me and released the holding mechanism. The rocket spewed water and air all over me, and went flying fifty feet into the air. Jason screamed with delight, ran over to our driveway, and retrieved the rocket for the third time. Our front yard was big enough to handle the trajectory if the rocket were to go straight up and down, which it had thus far.

"Come on, Dad, really pump it hard this time. I want to see it disappear into the clouds."

"OK, Son, but look around to make sure that no jets are flying less than 30,000 feet so we don't kill anyone."

Not understanding it was a joke, he carefully scanned the blue sky for any unsuspecting pilot not ready to meet his Maker.

"OK, Dad, I don't see any jets. Go ahead!"

This time I pumped on the handle about twenty-five times. Water was beginning to spew from the pressure chamber so I repeated the launching procedure. A gust of wind passed by at the precise moment that I launched the rocket. The wind carried the rocket over the front yard and house. Jason and I went into the backyard to look for the rocket but the wind had carried it over the backyard fence. It was gone.

"Let's go get it, Dad."

"Son, we can't. I can't walk through the field."

There was no way to retrieve it without going into a rough field with very high grass that lay behind the fence. We didn't have a gate that led to the field. It had just rained so my wheelchair would get stuck in the mud. Even if I could get to the field and try to walk through the mud, high grass, and potholes, I would have to walk well over 300 yards to get to the rocket. My previous record was less than that distance, and that was before my second back surgery.

Jason acted like it didn't matter and began playing with something else. I sat there thinking of all of the possible ways to retrieve the rocket and they were all unreasonable to get a rocket worth two dollars. I went back into the house, but the rocket haunted me. At work I couldn't concentrate on anything because of that stupid rocket. Several days passed and it only got worse. Almost a week later I was in the backyard pushing Jason and Jonathan on the swings. No matter which way I faced I couldn't ignore that fence. It was a constant reminder of my handicap. I decided to go inside. I would not be forced into facing my shortcomings. I was halfway to the door when I stopped. I couldn't stand it anymore. I began beating my wheelchair with my fists. Anger was welling up inside of me. I was beginning to hurt my hands but I didn't care. I just kept hitting it.

"Dad, what's wrong?" Jason asked, running over to me with an innocent look on his face. I turned around and faced the fence that was causing my frustrations.

"It's that rocket, Son. I want to go get it, but I can't. I just can't walk that far."

"Yes, you can, Dad. You can do anything," he said with stars in his eyes as if I were Superman, the Hulk, and He-man all rolled into one. I knew that the most important thing in the world right at that moment was to keep those stars in his eyes. I didn't ever want to see the look of disappointment that I had seen in them the day we looked through *The Daddy Book* together. I knew he understood that there were some things that I couldn't do, but to quit before trying would be a terrible example for both of my sons.

"You're right, Jason, I CAN."

We went into the house and I put my braces on. I didn't know how I was going to get that rocket, but I knew I was going to die trying. I went out of the front yard and down the block in my chair with Jason singing war songs as if we were going to fight. Ten minutes later, I was at the beginning of the field. I began pushing my chair through the high grass and mud. Twenty feet later, my wheelchair was stuck. I got my crutches and began to walk very slowly through the grass and mud holes. After fifty yards, I was exhausted. I rested for awhile and started again. I knew if I fell so soon after my recent surgery, I could be in real trouble so I just didn't think about it. Now over halfway there, I struggled on with frequent rest stops. Jason walked ahead and began to play on top of a huge pile of freshly moved dirt. I was not paying very close attention to him or I would have noticed what had put the pile there. Suddenly he screamed and ran back to me, he was covered with fire ants that were biting him all over. I tried to brush some of them off, but I was so unstable, I couldn't really reach anything other than his head.

"Wanice!" I screamed several times toward our backyard still over fifty yards away. Finally her head popped over the back yard fence and I told her what was wrong. She jumped the fence, ran over and brushed most of them off, and took him home to get him out of his clothes. They disappeared over the fence and I kept going. No matter what happened, I was going to get that rocket.

Soon I came to a grade too steep for me to climb. I fell forward slowly and began crawling up the embankment on my face. Pulling my crutches behind me, I crawled until I came to an ant bed. Now what? My only hope was to get up on my knees and try to crawl like a baby over the ant bed. I tried pushing myself up to my knees. Somehow, I did it. I began crawling like my one-year-old. I was doing it! I slowly made my way over to our fence and used it to stand up. I brushed some of the dirt, grass, and ants off. I began walking again beyond all logical strength barriers. I looked as I approached the area where the rocket should have been, but I couldn't see it for the tall grass. But you know what? It didn't matter anymore whether I found the rocket or not. What mattered is that I had tried. I walked slowly back to my wheelchair, taking over an hour. I rolled back home satisfied with the knowledge that I hadn't let Jason down and I had just walked more than two times farther than my previous record. Soon after I bought Jason a new rocket. But all he talked about was the day he and his dad walked through the field together. The stars stayed in his eyes and I was determined to keep them there.

I began recommitting myself to the Miracle Walk. Jim and I started lifting weights and walking every other night without fail. I couldn't work out too hard because of the recent surgery and body jacket, but I lifted as much as I could. I mainly began concentrating on extending the distance I was walking currently. My first goal was one mile with no time limit. This distance was a drop in the bucket compared to twenty-four miles, so I didn't think about the magnitude of the eventual goal. I just concentrated all of my effort on my first goal. Slowly I added to the distance one painful step at a time. My legs were not getting appreciably bigger or stronger. However the more I walked, the easier it became. I also noticed that my hypersensitivity was growing much worse. What I learned later was that a medical miracle was taking place. Dr. Wharton's brilliant surgery had fused my spine far better than before and was taking pressure off of my spinal cord. This meant more pain to my legs but it also meant additional leg movement was returning. It wasn't nearly enough to walk without braces, but it did mean that my legs could take more of my weight off of my arms. Was this an answer to prayer or just good surgery? I believe it was both.

On October 15, 1983, I walked one mile. When I walked back through the door, Wanice had both of the kids waiting for me at the front door. Everyone was cheering. If I hadn't realized it before, I knew it then that Wanice was behind me and the Miracle Walk 100 percent. It was the most physically exhausting thing I had ever done in my life. It left me without any energy at all. I wondered how I was ever going to be able to walk a farther distance. But I wasn't discouraged and set two miles for my next goal.

One night while reading the Scriptures I stumbled across a passage that I had never quite understood. I was reading the story of Gideon. He was facing the Midianites who had 30,000 men. Gideon had a force of 3,000 men, but he was confident in God's deliverance and power. Gideon was ready to go into battle and give God all of the praise and glory for the victory; however God told him that even though he was so outnumbered, it was possible for the Israelites to still give themselves credit for the victory. So God and Gideon began to eliminate many of the men through a series of tests. Now all that remained were 300 men to fight 30,000. God declared that then no one could doubt it was God's battle—not man's. So, people could not take credit.

Suddenly it occurred to me what had happened in my life in the past three months. I had said that I was prepared to do something which I felt was impossible and to give God the glory. God had said "OK" to me, but the odds were still too much in my favor, so He reduced my chances of doing this alone. He allowed the enemy to depress me about work, I had another painful back operation, my feet were burned, friends and fellow Christians had turned on me, you name it. I saw it for the first time as a test of my ability to trust God at His Word. It reminded me that God was the same yesterday as He is today. What He did with the biblical characters, He does with us today. I became excited about what God was about to do in my life. If I wanted more faith, I was going to have to increase my trust in God.

The following Sunday was Harvest Sunday at Southcliff Baptist

Church. Once a year our church gathered together for a special service centered on giving. All of the offerings were to go to debt retirement of our old building loans. Wanice and I were talking about what we could afford to give under the circumstances of my coming layoff. We prayed about the figure which was small and wrote the check. The whole family piled in the car and off we went to the morning worship time. Our guest preacher Jack Taylor delivered a message on giving. He urged us to give, keeping in mind that we can't outgive God. The more we give, the more God gives to us in return.

I turned to Wanice and whispered, "Honey, I don't think our gift is big enough. If we want God to help me in my job situation, we have to show Him that we trust in Him, not our finances."

"Well, how much did you have in mind?"

I whispered the amount that I felt would show our dependence on God. She almost fell over in the pew.

"Are you sure?" she asked after she had pulled herself together. I nodded and she wrote the check.

It was amazing how fast circumstances changed at work. Suddenly it seemed that I had the key to success. Everything I touched at work turned to gold. They began sending me on field trips to Michigan, Wyoming, and several through Texas. Every time I went to the field to run a production log, I was the recipient of many curious eyes. While the average oil-field hand looks like "Mr. T," I really stood out in a wheelchair and braces. I had the opportunity to share my faith in Christ with many curious oil-field workers. I received a letter of commendation from the vice-president of the Wireline Division. My boss signed it, and told me that I had a brilliant future with Pengo. I learned the most important words in a person's faith were, "Trust in God's Word".

The months passed quickly, and soon it was fall. Jim and I were still working out every other day, but I could not involve myself in any serious workouts or racing with the body jacket still in place. I waited patiently, knowing that with each passing day, I was closer to the day I would walk twenty-four miles. I was adding to my walking distance and was up to two grueling miles that hurt me everywhere I could feel. I was looking forward to the day the body jacket would come off, and I could really push myself. I tried not to get discouraged about my progress. I knew that where my body failed along the Miracle Walk, God would carry me the rest of the way as He had promised in my vision six months before.

14
In Training

On Christmas Day, 1983, I removed the body jacket I had worn for six long months. Not wearing it felt wonderful! I was free to move again. I got down on the floor with the kids and played with their new toys. They loved having me on the floor with them and I crawled around as they jumped on top of me. They enjoyed having a dad who could do so much more with them. They just kept hugging and kissing me. I promised Wanice that I wouldn't put too much strain on my back until I was accustomed to having the body jacket off. Even though I was anxious to start training for the walk, I didn't start lifting weights until the holidays were over.

My longest walk had been two miles at this point. I was concerned about my progress but I tried not to worry and just trust in God's promise. I was going to have to continue to trust Him. On January 4, 1984, I officially started training for the Miracle Walk that was now exactly six months away. To evaluate my physical progress, I measured my arms and chest. My upper arms were fifteen inches in the flexed position, my chest was forty-four inches around, and my forearms were thirteen inches. My good friend Jim Hurst came over religiously every other day to help me work out. Both he and his wife Jane believed in the Miracle Walk even though there was little evidence to prove that it was going to be successful. I learned a lot about servanthood through their lives. On the first night, I began lifting 150 pounds on the bench press and was exhausted after only a few repetitions. Jim and I both participated in a game we made up called the bench-press marathon. This is how it worked. If we could lift it more than five times, we increased the weight ten pounds. Then we took off ten pounds on each repetition until we were down to the bar itself. By that time, we had trouble lifting our arms, much less the bar.

I also built a set of parallel bars in my garage with pipes from a hardware store. At first I could only lift myself about twenty times. That was a far cry from the fifty parallel-bar body lifts I had managed to do in the rehabilitation center. I set a goal of fifty lifts. Jim and I started the first of the most serious, muscle-tearing, bone-wrenching, heart-pounding work-outs in which we had ever participated. I concentrated on training for the walk in my wheelchair because I found that when I walked too much, the braces caused sores to develop on my feet and legs. I was going to have to develop my strength with weights and increase my endurance with the racing wheelchair. In my eyes, the secret was not to *be able* to walk that far, but to be *strong* enough to walk the distance. My actual strength and endurance in walking were going to be theoretically realized, not actually realized until the day of the Miracle Walk. My legs and feet couldn't handle that kind of punishment more than once.

Within months, I was able to lift 225 pounds on the bench press at least ten times. I was curling a thirty-five pound dumbbell with each arm at least thirty times. (In the sitting position, that wasn't easy.) Jim and I set various goals for ourselves, and we began meeting them one by one. I was up to twelve miles on the chair at a fast speed. In the mile, I was pushing my chair at a pace of less than five-and-a-half minutes. I would push my chair faster and faster until I thought my heart would stop and my lungs would burst, then I would go a little farther.

Everything was going well with our training program except for my parallel-bar dips. I was stuck in the forty-repetition range, and I could not seem to do any more. The weeks dragged on and I was getting no-where. It was so frustrating; but I had set a goal that I felt was realistic and I was not going to give up until I reached it.

The farthest that I had walked was three-and-one-half miles, after which I was thoroughly exhausted. My feet began to break down so I decided that I was working too much in the braces and not enough on weights and in the chair. It did concern me though, that my feet and legs began to bleed in such a short distance compared to the goal that lay before me, but I trusted that God would work that out, too.

Along with preparing myself physically, I wanted to be prepared spiri-tually for the doubts and frustrations that would befall me as I continued toward the eventual goal. I outlined a goal-accomplishing method to which I would adhere to throughout the training and walk. At first it was a rough outline, until I was inspired much later to put it into steps that others might follow.

1. *The dream:* God put the dream in my heart that I could believe in and hold onto through the hard times.

2. *The desire:* the passion to follow God and make the dream come true.

3. *The proper faith:* believing more in God than in the plan and believing that He will carry you through the rough times.

4. *Problem solving:* manage new problems that arise knowing that God has them all in His hands. The enemy will attack, but don't get discouraged.

5. *Paying the price:* God allows us to be tested by fire as we reach our goal. Remember that just like gold, our faith is purified by fire.

6. *Waiting on the Lord:* it is very difficult not to give up at this point. After having done all you can do, it's His turn. The key is trust!

7. *Praising the Lord:* Praising God regardless of what is happening around you, expect the result that He has promised.

8. *Giving God the Glory:* After accomplishing the goal, give God the Glory for the things He has done. Here is where most of us fail. If we set a goal too short, the goal was probably accomplished by us, not God.

In March of 1984, Wanice and I flew out to California on business. We were met at the Airport by Bob and Ruthie Peterson who drove us straight to Rancho Los Amigos. I wanted to show Beth my progress. I prayed all the way there that I would be able to talk with her without any bitterness. I especially didn't want to come across as if I were saying, "I told you I could do it." I was so nervous as I walked across the parking lot into the hospital. It was not until then that I realized just how far I had come. It just didn't seem real that I was actually walking back into Rancho. When I left, I had been totally dependent on the chair.

As soon as I walked into my old ward building, I was surrounded by nurses and aides who remembered me. There was hugging and kissing everywhere. They were all shocked beyond words at my progress; however, my real appointment at Rancho was in physical therapy. It was about lunchtime, and I was told that the therapists were outside barbecuing for the patients. I saw Beth as soon as I walked outside. She was about thirty feet away with her back to me. I walked about ten steps and then called her.

"Beth!"

I could tell by the way she was slowly turning around that she had recognized my voice. As she pivoted slowly, her eyes popped open.

"Rob? I can't believe it. Look at you walk!"

I walked the rest of the way over to her and she gave me a big hug. I was surprised but happy that she was glad to see me. She asked me several questions about my new braces. She was impressed with how light they appeared to be. She avoided any reference to our difficulties in the past. She was either making an attempt to ask forgiveness or it was the best act I had ever seen. She acted thrilled to see me. I was so glad that our meeting went well. I told her that I attributed my recovery to hard work and prayer. She agreed that something had definitely happened during the short year I was gone. Soon after, Bob, Ruthie, Wanice, and I walked back out to the car where I was about to face a part of my past. It caused me realize how thankful I should be, and to whom I should be thankful.

After we were in the car and ready to leave, I saw a familiar person roll by in his wheelchair. It was Mike. He was the young man who started ambulation trials on the same day as I. I remembered how Beth had told me that he had a far greater chance of walking because he was younger and lighter. I was anxious to talk with him about his progress. I asked Bob to stop by the car that Eddy was getting into. "Eddy! Remember me? It's Rob Bryant."

"Oh yeah. Hi, Rob, how are you doing?"

" I'm just fine. I'm walking farther and farther. As a matter of fact, I have walked over three miles nonstop."

I could tell by his reaction that I was saying the wrong thing. So I stopped talking about myself.

"How about you? Are you walking? Are you moving your legs at all?" I asked. After looking down at his legs, the answer was obvious. They had atrophied down to skin and bones.

"No, I gave it up. It was too hard," he said, looking away and getting into his car. I wished that I had never asked, but the damage was already done. I couldn't take my words back. I said good-bye and we left for Camarillo. All the way there I just thought about Mike and hoped that maybe he would try again now, knowing it was possible with hard work. But the more I thought about it, I realized that all of the hard work in the world won't rejuvenate nerves as had happened to me. It was pure grace and I should be ever mindful from where my blessings had come. There would be no way for me to take one step, without God's help. According to Beth, walking for me was impossible.

Soon we arrived in Camarillo. The whole Pleasant Valley gang threw a big homecoming party for us that night at Jeff and Judy Wilson's house. It was great to see everyone again. No one could believe the progress I had made in the year that I had been away. I was determined to not use my wheelchair at all during the long weekend in order to continue my training while not able to lift weights. Bob and Jeff took me with them to see the beach and the California scenery. I grew tired quickly, but I kept going. Before I realized it, I had walked several miles with them.

On Sunday, I did something that I promised myself that I would do someday. I walked down the aisle of the church at the pastor's invitation and shared with the congregation what the Lord had laid on my heart to share that day. I talked about what God had done in my life during the year since I had been away and then I left them with this thought.

"If God in His wisdom allows something precious to you to be taken away, there is a reason. You might or might not learn the reason but I think the important aspect of the loss is how we react to the crisis. If a Christian's foundation falls apart when something is taken away, he didn't have the right foundation in the first place. God promises that no matter what happens, He won't give us any more than we can handle, and if we build our lives on the rock (Jesus) nothing can shake us. We are living in a lost and dying world. When we crumble like sand, the world watches and is reassured that we don't have any answers either. Be thankful for what you have and not bitter for what you have lost. God bless you."

After the service, Wanice and I talked with many of our friends that we had come to know during our short stay in California a year before. Everyone gave us a hug and wished us well. On the following day, we flew back to Texas. During the two days I had walked in California, I had begun to wear a bad sore on my right foot, but I didn't say anything to anyone about it. It only grew worse as time went on. I didn't walk for a couple of weeks, hoping it would go away.

In April, a friend of mine suggested that I contact a few nonprofit organizations to see if I could raise money for them during the walk with pledges per mile. I thought that would be a great idea, and perhaps I could help others while following this dream of mine. After contacting a few agencies, I called the American Paralysis Association. I spoke with the president, Kent Waltrep. He was very interested and wanted to speak with me. I learned all about the research, experimental projects, and testing that they were funding to find a cure for accidental paralysis victims. I also learned more about what an inspiration Kent Waltrep had been to millions around the Dallas/Fort Worth area. He had been a running back for Texas Christian University in Fort Worth until his accident in 1975, which left him a quadriplegic (paralyzed from the neck down). He didn't give up. After a few years of trying to get the kind of therapy that today's technology had to offer, he founded the American Paralysis Association. His kind of determination was new to me and I wanted to be associated with his winner attitude. We both decided that I should walk for the American Paralysis Association. In May, I began passing out pledge sheets all over the country, from California to New York. Pledges were pouring in from everywhere. Within weeks we were into the thousands of dollars. I assigned some friends to the task of helping raise money while I continued to prepare myself for the ordeal now just six weeks away.

Meanwhile, the sore on my foot was not going away, so I went to DRI to see my doctor and therapist about it. They could see right away that it was a decubitus sore (a sore that starts at the bone and works out) and were concerned about it. Dr. Wharton advised me either not to walk as much or, even better, to stay off of it for one month. If I continued walking, Dr. Wharton warned, I could lose my foot.

I knew he was right and I respected his medical advice, but I couldn't turn back now. I was committed. I decided that I was going to continue with my plans but that I would have to reduce the pressure on the area. That's when I got an idea that was the best of both worlds. I had orthotics put a piece of plastazote (soft rubberized material) around the area. When I got home I took a doorknob cutter and cut a hole right through the brace at the sore area. Then I sanded the plastazote down to a smooth surface that contoured my skin. The plastazote prohibited the edge of the circle I had cut out from rubbing on skin. Next I removed the sharp edges of the cut brace with a rasp file. I put the brace on and it fit perfectly. Now I could walk with the sore exposed to the air and no pressure was being exerted upon it. One week before the walk, I went back to DRI to get my sore examined one more time. The Doctor couldn't believe the swelling had gone down so quickly. He thought that I had stopped walking altogether. I showed the brace adjustment I had made to the orthotics specialist. He said that if the adjustment really worked, he was going to perform similar operations for some of his other patients. He said he was going to call it "The Bryant Technique."

Only two obstacles remained, besides the obvious problem of not being able to walk that far on my own ability. First of all, I still had not yet reached fifty dips on the parallel bars. I felt that was essential to my confidence that I accomplish this one last goal. With just two weeks to go, I kept trying. The second obstacle was finding enough people who were free at the required times to accompany me all the way along the twenty-four-mile route. I knew the walk was going to take three days, so I needed a total of six people to walk along with me. I figured two fresh people per day would be required. I didn't want to ask any person to walk more than one day because I wanted everyone to be wide awake and free from any heat prostration. I expected the temperature to be in the low 100s. I didn't want anyone who was out of shape to keel over due to the heat. But God had that worked out in a manner I never would have expected. Just one week before the walk, my phone rang.

"Hello, Rob. This is Jeff Wilson and Bob Peterson calling from good old Southern California. We were just talking with our wives about this dream of yours and we want to be there to see it through with you," Jeff said with a friendly voice.

"You guys are too much, you have already helped me in too many ways to count. I can't think of anyone I would rather have walk with me. You guys really understand what I have been through these past eighteen months. Besides it was your wives that were outside the room the day the doctor told me I would never walk again. Somehow it seems right that it be you guys who walk along with me to see it all come true. I do want to warn you about something, though. I expect it to be very hot. Do you think you can be fresh enough on the second and third day to watch the traffic and lead me on the safest and easiest paths?"

"Well, both of us were hoping we could come and have been working out to get ready by running, riding bikes, and so forth. We are ready and eager to do whatever is required of us," Bob said. We continued to discuss their arrival time, what they should bring with them and all the little details of their visit. They would arrive during the afternoon of June 30th. I was so excited I couldn't stand it. It was too good to be true! I would have Jim walk along as my trainer and these two close friends for moral support and logistics.

The remaining days flew by and I continued my training after work. By then the pledges toward the walk were over 9,000 dollars. On Friday, June thirtieth, my office at Pengo wished me well. Many of them prayed with me that I would have victory in a seemingly impossible task.

On Saturday afternoon, Wanice and I drove to the airport to pick up Jeff and Bob. It was great seeing them. We talked all the way home about the logistics of the walk. Jeff was an engineer for the navy, so he had all of the technical details worked out as far as the placement of the car, using a bike for a forerunner, and many other aspects. He became our trouble shooter and worked out the problems as they arose. Bob was the greatest source of encouragement that I could have had. He never said *never.* He made me think I could do it, like the little locomotive who thought he could. With the combination of these two diverse personalities, the prospect of victory was increased in my mind. But with the faith that the three of us together had in God, we knew that wherever my strength failed, God was going to carry me the rest of the way.

Jim and I had one last workout on Saturday night, now just two days from the Miracle Walk. We both knew what had to be done that night. I worked out briefly with the dumbbells and on my leg lifts. Then I turned and faced the parallel bars. Jim watched me out of the corner of his eye. We both knew that psychologically I needed this small victory. I rolled slowly over to the bars knowing that the time had come. I was going to do it. Jim walked over to the bars without a word. I could tell he was praying. He reached down and placed my legs in the strap. I pushed my weight up on top of the bars with my arms. I started. Jim counted out loud.

"One, two, three, four, five . . ." he counted as I found a rhythm that was comfortable. I was not going to come down off the bars until I heard Jim say that magic number, "Fifty."

"Twenty-one, twenty-two, twenty-three," he counted with a growing excitement in his voice. I didn't feel tired at all. Normally about then I would start to fatigue.

"Thirty-one, thirty-two," he continued counting, giving me a knowing look. I was starting to feel the tightness begin then, but my adrenalin started pumping and I kept going.

"Forty-one, forty-two, forty-three," Jim counted, searching my eyes to see how I was doing. A tiny smile crept across his face. I slowed to a crawl, but I refused to admit defeat.

"Forty-five, forty-six, forty-seven," his voice boomed with anticipation. "Forty-eight, forty-nine," he said as I went down for the last one. Everything was gone, and I knew it. This last one was going to have to come from the heart. I began to push my way up that final time. Jim was crouching at the knees slightly and was standing up slowly as if to help me push.

"Come on, Rob, you can do it," he yelled, clenching his fists and encouraging me. I kept pushing and somehow I found enough strength to get to the top.

"Fifty!" we both screamed together. I fell down into my wheelchair with a thud as we continued to shout with joy. I caught my breath just as Bob and Jeff came into the garage and celebrated the victory with us. Now that my training program was complete, we measured my arms. They were a staggering seventeen inches around. They had increased more than two inches in size. My chest was forty-six inches around, growing more than three inches. That last night before the Miracle Walk I ate enough calories and protein to give power to a rocket ship. Wanice fed me every high-energy, low-sugar food she could think of. The table looked like Thanksgiving Dinner. I ate until I thought I would burst. I was going to need all of the energy I could get.

Everything I could think of was taken care of. I was as ready as I could be for the Miracle Walk. Now the rest was up to God!

15
The Miracle Walk

Day One

Buzzzz. My alarm started ringing at 4:25 AM. Wanice rolled over and turned off the alarm.

"Rob, are you awake?" she asked me in a whisper.

"Yes! Go wake up Bob and Jeff while I start dressing."

I could hear Bob and Jeff talking quietly in the other room and could tell by their voices that they were just as excited about all of this as I was. During the night they had worked out a plan as to who was going to grab what in the morning as they packed the car with crutches, extra braces, my wheelchair, our snacks, and water.

It was as if they had done this sort of thing many times before. I put on my braces, checked the rubber padding I had put on the handles of my crutches, and packed two different kinds of gloves. We all finished our various projects just as Wanice was putting oatmeal, toast, cereal and juices on the table. I wasn't hungry considering what I had eaten the night before and considering my excited state, but I knew I would need all of the help I could get. After breakfast the three of us climbed into my car and we were off. Twenty minutes later, we were at the starting point and the Miracle Walk began at 6:35 AM on July 2.

I picked up a fast pace and was off to the races. Considering my longest walk to date had been three-and-one-half miles, I had a long way to go in a very short time. I would have to walk eight times farther and maintain as good a time for three straight days as I had for the three-and-a-half miles. This was going to take a miracle and I knew it. We rested at the first stop point which was exactly a mile and a half. I glanced at my watch. It was 7:55 AM. That was a good time, but I couldn't afford to slow down if I wanted to finish one third of the walk by nightfall. Jeff and Bob checked my legs for any sore places. Finding none, I was off again.

Jeff moved the car to the next rest stop at the three-mile marker and rode his bike back. By doing this, I could always rest in the car at each rest stop. Also Jeff ("Tonto" as we came to call him) could scout out the terrain up ahead for any would-be problems.

By 9:00, the temperature was already starting to climb, but it was cloudy with a slight breeze, so it was bearable. We weren't sure how I did it, but I walked the next mile and a half in under one hour. I still was not feeling fatigued. However, one aspect of the walk I had not anticipated was the tilted angle of the shoulder of the road. The angle was barely noticeable, but in order to compensate for it, I was having to lean to the left on each stride. This began bothering my back and left shoulder. I tried walking on the opposite shoulder but this was even worse. So I crossed the road again and tried to ignore the growing pain in my back and shoulder. Jim and Jay joined us several times along the way. Jim had to work all day but he left the office several times to check up on us.

By 12 noon, I had walked a torturous six-and-one-half miles. Wanice joined us for lunch at a pizza place. I stuffed myself on pizza and drank plenty of water. The temperature was close to one hundred already so the car's air-conditioning felt good. After we ate I tried to get up but the air conditioning had caused my hot, sweaty muscles to cramp. They helped me outside and I rested, allowing the warm air to loosen my muscles again. I was developing a sore below my knee where a strap was rubbing it. While I continued to rest, Bob and Jeff acted as a racing crew—changing my sweaty socks, checking for more sores, and rubbing my already-stiff hands. I switched gloves for the first time. The first pair were weight-lifting gloves which were soft in the palm area. The second pair were wheelchair gloves which had a thick rubber pad on the palms. By changing gloves, I effectively moved the pressure points around.

At 1:30 PM, I was off again, but this time I moved significantly slower. I could see Jeff's concern at my new pace. But after an hour or so, I was moving a little faster. I began hitting a few small hills for the first time during the walk. They were barely noticeable to a car, but to me on my braces they were like small mountains. On flat surfaces, I could use my body weight as momentum to fall forward and catch myself with the next leg and crutch, much like an able-bodied person does without crutches. But on the hills, I could not lean any farther than my braced shoes would allow, since I could not bend at the ankles. Each step was a concentrated effort and I could not use momentum. My stride was much jerkier and required more effort then did a smooth gait.

The sore below my right knee was growing worse. We examined it at each rest stop. That's when Jeff got an idea. "What if we put a knee pad directly on the sore and the strap over that? That way it can't rub you anymore and it will distribute the pressure exerted by the brace strap," Jeff said with typical engineer's logic.

"That just might work," I replied, and Wanice went off to buy one while I finished my break. When she returned, we tried it. It worked great. Now at least I didn't have to worry about infections or pressure sores.

I stopped at each mile marker. By 2:30 PM, I had walked a total of seven-and-one-half miles. I took a fifteen-minute break that seemed like five and was off again. I was really growing tired at that point. Each step was a conscious act of will. I had to keep telling myself. "One more step, each step is one closer to Keist Park." Bob and Jeff began to encourage me on. I was tired and sore everywhere I could feel, but I wasn't giving up. Far too much prayer, training, and planning had gone into this to give up now. I came to the foot of a large hill a half hour later and ran out of energy. There was nothing left. My strength and courage ran out simultaneously and I knew I was through for the day. The ninety-eight-degree heat had sapped all of the "I-can" attitude out of me. It was 3:30 in the afternoon. I hated to waste daylight but if I wanted to walk the next day, I was going to have to quit now. I felt so disappointed that I had not made my goal of eight-and-one-half miles for the first day. If I expected to complete this walk, I was going to have to make goals and stick to them, but I couldn't make it up another hill. By then Jim and Wanice were there with their cars so I got into Jim's car and Bob and Jeff got in with Wanice. Jim pulled out of the driveway we were in and out onto the road. I couldn't believe my eyes.

"Jim, look, there it is. The eight-and-one-half mile marker. We made it. God gave me the strength to reach our goal and we didn't even know it. God carried me to my first goal. I wonder where my strength ran out today and His began?"

"I don't know, but I do know that you and God can do anything He wants you to!"

When I arrived at home, I took a quick bath which took so much energy that I was afraid I wouldn't be able to transfer back into the wheelchair. After fifteen minutes of struggle, I made it. Wanice served up another huge meal of carbohydrates. I was so tired I could barely eat. It was then that I realized that I needed some prayer in order to even consider getting up the next morning and try walking for another day. After calling a few friends and asking them to come over and pray with me, I went into the living room and rested. Bob and Jeff rubbed my sore hands and examined my open sore below my right knee. It looked pretty bad.

In the meantime, Bob and Jeff answered the phone and helped Wanice clear the table. They were incredible. Jeff even made some signs for our backs. I was so glad that they had come. My admiration for those two men was growing by the minute. They, like Jim, were demonstrating a servant's heart. Each one of them called home to tell their wives about the day, but I could tell there was a great deal of concern about how I was going to be able to finish two more days of this extreme physical exertion. But they didn't burden me with their worries. They just prayed.

About an hour later, people started arriving and they began to pray with me. After forming a circle around me, everyone got on their knees. One by one, they prayed for my strength to return in the morning. By nine PM, they were leaving and I crawled into bed to sleep for seven hours. I dreamed all night about walking. My legs were having severe spasms as a result of the day's work. I kept waking up feeling as if I hadn't been asleep at all.

Day Two

BUZZZZZ...

"Rob, are you awake? It's 4:30!"

"Yes, let's do it just like yesterday morning."

She got up and woke Bob and Jeff. I could hear Bob from my room. He growled like a bear when Wanice tried to wake him, but she just laughed at him. I was dressed in half an hour. I was surprised at how fresh I was. I thought that I would be much more tired. By 5:30 we were all having breakfast together. Jeff commented that I looked better than Bob did. We all laughed and decided that Bob was not a morning person. By 6, we were in the car and at 6:30 we were at the bottom of the hill that I would need to climb. I was anxious to see how much slower I was the second day than the first.

"Well, here goes," I said, standing up. Suddenly a sharp pain hit me in my groin above my left leg. It was so tight. I stretched it a few times and the pain lessened. While Jeff and Bob looked on with concern, I started walking. The pain slowly went away and I started up the hill. It didn't look nearly as steep as it had the day before. Within half an hour I was at the top, and I didn't even feel as if I had walked the previous day. *Prayer works wonders,* I thought. But what I saw disturbed me. The general trend for the entire day was up. It wasn't a very steep grade, but it was noticeable. I tried not to think about it. I just thought about all of the prayers that were prayed the night before. *Just worry about getting to the next stopping point,* I would tell myself. So Jim, Jay, Bob, Jeff, and I took one step at a time, one mile at a time, and one break at a time, knowing we had the faith to hang on for another mile. I began taking breaks every mile instead of every mile and a half, like the day before. I was able to keep my speed up to almost a mile an hour, but I just couldn't walk as far before I gave out.

At the third rest stop, a car pulled up and two men got out. One had a camera and the other had a note pad. The first set of reporters had arrived. While one took pictures, the other asked every question imaginable. After fifteen minutes Jeff looked at his watch and told me that we had better go.

Jeff and Bob changed my socks, checked my legs for sores, rubbed my aching hands, and we were off again. The reporters walked along for fifteen or twenty minutes asking additional questions, then left to meet a deadline. At around noon we stopped for lunch at a restaurant that was along the way. It couldn't have come a moment too soon. I was beginning to drag my right leg. I was exactly halfway, with four more miles to go after lunch. While we were eating, another friend showed up with a video camera to make a video of the remainder of the walk. He ate with us. I ate a big meal, then started eating from everyone else's plate. I just couldn't get enough.

After lunch we went out to the car and took another break. I fell fast asleep and they decided to let me sleep for an hour. At 1:30 they woke me up and we were off again. But I was really tired. Now both of my legs were tight and my arms and back were sore. I was so glad that I had worked out as hard as I had. Now if my severely handicapped legs could just keep up with my huge shoulders. I began stopping every three quarters of a mile at that point. That was at the outside edge of my endurance and it was all I could do to get from break to break. My breaks were starting to be twenty minutes instead of fifteen. It was taking longer and longer for me to recover from the previous short walk.

As we made our way to the next rest stop, I saw people waving and honking their car horns. I figured our story must have been on a lot of different radio stations.

After the next break, the road finally assumed a flat grade and I could see a lake in the distance which would mark the end of the walk for the day. My hypersensitive leg hurt so bad that I was close to tears. Each stride made my pants rub against my inner thigh. It felt like a fire burning my leg but I tried not to think about it. Besides, I was hurting all over; my leg was just one more place. Slowly another mile went by and the road started to dip down toward the lake. We cut across a supermarket parking lot and I walked past a gas station. One of the mechanics saw us, got out from under a car, and walked over to me.

"Are you Rob Bryant?" he asked, wiping the grease off of his hand onto his trousers.

"Yes," I answered and introduced the rest of the gang. "I heard about what you are doing on the radio this morning. I can't believe you are attempting to walk so far. I want you to know it is a pleasure to meet you. You have given me courage to face my problems with determination. If you can handle your problems, I can sure handle mine. Can I do anything for you?"

"Well, to tell you the truth, I have been drinking nothing but Gatorade to maintain adequate electro-lite fluids and minerals in my system to deal with this tremendous heat. We are almost out. Do you have any?"

He nodded and signaled me to wait. In less than a minute he reappeared and gave Bob about ten free cans of Gatorade. We all said goodbye and we were off again. In less than an hour we were at the lake. I swallowed several aspirins to help block out some of the pain from my legs, back, arms, and hands. My hands had deep bruises in them and were turning a reddish purple. The problem was that I had to lift at least half of my weight on each stride in order to move my legs forward. My hands were taking a tremendous beating, and were beginning to tingle with numbness. I hoped that I was not doing any permanent damage.

We decided that I had better walk another mile on the other side of the lake so I would have less to walk on the following day. I was supposed to finish at 2:00 in Keist Park the following day. With eight miles to go, Jeff figured I would need to average more than a mile an hour if I stopped at the lake. We drove across the lake and I walked one more hot, painful mile. I remembered my first mile less than a year in the past. Remembering Wanice's and the kids' faces at the door cheering me on gave me the strength to finish for the day. At the end of the mile, I collapsed in the car. Another day of the Miracle Walk had come to an end. It was after 6:30 PM.

"You know that we have to be back here in less than twelve hours from now to do this again."

"Don't depress me with the facts. Let's go home," Bob said. We packed up our gear and drove away.

At home it was a madhouse. The phone was ringing with reporters calling. Many concerned friends were calling. Bob and Jeff were such a terrific help at taking care of the phone and helping Wanice with dinner. By 8:00, I had already taken a shower, had my wounds doctored and was in bed. Bob and Jeff just ran around preparing everything for the next day. I was so glad that they had come. My legs were spasming badly and the pain was terrific, but I was too tired to care. By 9:00, I was fast asleep and dreaming about walking across that finish line on the following day.

Day Three

By the third day we had the routine down so when the alarm went off at four AM we were ready to go by 5:30. I felt as if I had been hit by a truck. I had no energy left. My motivation was gone. Bob went outside and brought in the paper to see if the newspaper had printed our story. We almost fell over when we read in big letters on the front page: MAN LEANS ON FAITH IN HIS MIRACLE WALK. There it was! Could it be that I was really going to be able to complete this thing. Suddenly I was filled with energy and we were on the road to the final stretch. We arrived at 6:15 AM and I stretched my sore stiff legs.

"I've got an idea. Why don't you guys take turns carrying me this morning. Who wants to be first?" I asked.

Everyone laughed and I was off again. I was walking slowly and noticeably dragging my right leg with each stride. I just prayed that God would give me the strength to make it to the next break point. I blocked out the pain by listening to a radio. I listened to some of the largest radio stations in Dallas and I heard most of them say something about my walk and what time I was supposed to finish. At around 9 AM a photographer from United Press International stopped me and took pictures that would be immediately wired all across the country. I couldn't believe that the Miracle Walk was going to get such coverage. But why shouldn't I believe it? God had promised that if I remembered Him, He would remember me. Just in case I was tempted to pat myself on the back, I made a mental note that when I finished I was going to give all of the glory to God. By 11 AM, it was over 100 degrees and getting difficult to breath. At 11:30 we sighted a helicopter from one of the local radio stations. It flew over at least once an hour to keep track of my location.

By noon I arrived at the park. I looked at my watch. None of us could believe it. I had just walked six miles in six hours including two long breaks. Now all I had to do was walk around the park. My arrival time was to be 2:00 PM and I had a mile and a half to go. We stopped for lunch while Wanice and some of the others put up signs, and made a finish line tape for me to walk through at the center of the park. The park was getting crowded. Many people started to gather at the finish line to see what was going on. After lunch we started again. I was beyond exhaustion. I barely felt pain anymore as I was practically numb. The sore below my knee was a bright red despite the knee pad, but nothing was going to stop me now. I had heard of runners' talk about the "wall"—the point where a good runner will stop but a great runner will continue. It's when the pain is intolerable, all of the energy is gone, and your body is screaming to stop this madness; but the person just keeps on going despite the fact that he can't. That is what I felt as I was halfway around the park, but I kept walking. "Just one more step," I would tell myself. When I would finish that step I would tell myself, "Just one more step." And so I continued around three quarters of the park. I finally rested on a park bench with the end in sight. Was it true? Did I just walk twenty-four miles just one year from the day that I could walk only one block? I got up and started again with "Thank You, Jesus" coming out of my mouth with each step.

There it was up ahead—the finish line with friends, cameramen, reporters, and a small crowd. Suddenly with fifty yards to go, a TV camera positioned itself in front of me with a reporter asking me, *Why?* I began telling him of my struggle to walk again, of my faith in Jesus Christ—that He was the one who was worthy of praise and not me. Five minutes later I was approaching the tape, my emotions began to swell up within me. Jason and Jonathan ran up to me and gave me a hug as I approached the finish.

"I'm proud of you, Dad!" Jason said as he backed away for me to finish. I stopped for a second, then broke through the tape, and received cheers from the crowd. Right in the middle of the crowd was Kent Waltrep, President of the American Paralysis Association. I was ecstatic he had come to greet me at the finish line. I caught my breath for a moment and waited for the applause to stop. Jeff handed me a handmade replica of a check he had made. I turned to Kent. It suddenly became quiet. The only sounds were the cameras clicking and rolling.

"Kent, on behalf of all of the people who pledged money for this three-day Independence Day walk, I would like to present you with a check for 9,000 dollars. I do this in hope that the dollars raised here today will go toward research in finding a cure for accidental paralysis. I hope that one day you and I can walk without the aid of crutches, braces, and wheelchairs."

"Rob, I would like to present you with a plaque that will always commemorate this day. It says:

"IN APPRECIATION OF HIS COURAGE AND DETERMINATION, THE AMERICAN PARALYSIS ASSOCIATION HONORS ROB BRYANT FOR HIS INDEPENDENCE DAY WALK, JULY 4, 1984.

"Thank you for the inspiration that you have given to the hundreds of thousands that are in wheelchairs around the country. It is people like you that will give the rest us of the courage to face our problems regardless of what they are. Thank you for the money and rest assured that we will put it to good use."

With no strength left, I asked for my wheelchair. I sat down and the Miracle Walk was at long last over. God and I had done it. Kent and I began to talk as a few reporters gathered around to get the story. Kent mentioned to one of them that as far as he knew, this was the farthest that a paraplegic had ever walked. I tried to talk to Kent and answer all of the reporters' questions at one time. I introduced Jim Hurst, Jeff Wilson, Bob Peterson, and Jay Racz to the press. They were asked questions, too. After about a half an hour, Kent and I drove over to East Dallas to an APA fund-raiser that was going on at E-Systems of Dallas. Before a crowd of about 400 people, Kent again presented me with the plaque and I was asked to say a few words. I was so tired that I really don't remember much of what I said but I do remember saying this: "I want to give all of the praise and glory to God for making this walk possible. All of the hard work and determination will not rejuvenate nerves. I can move my left leg enough to walk some. But I believe it was God that gave me the strength to walk twenty-four miles. If courage is all it takes to walk after an injury like mine, Kent Waltrep would be walking, too. He certainly does not lack any determination. I also would like to thank my friends and especially my wife for believing in this dream of mine. Thank you all."

I again received a round of applause. Jeff, Bob, Wanice, and I visited with a few people who had questions about the walk, and then we went home. I collapsed into my easy chair. During the next few hours the phone rang off the wall with reporters. Cable News Network called and got an interview in which my voice was heard around the country on cable at six o'clock that night. The rest of the night passed quickly, we set off fireworks with some family and friends, and by ten I was in bed. Despite the pain, spasms, and excruciating hypersensitivity I slept well.

The following morning, I took Bob and Jeff to the airport. We said our good-byes and I waved as my two friends boarded the plane. During the drive home, I thought about when the Miracle Walk was only a dream. What if I had decided it was impossible, and it had merely remained a dream? I would never have developed my faith and God would not have blessed me with a miracle. *Godly Dreams*, I decided, *are to be realized, not merely fantasized.*

Little did I know that within two weeks I would speak to churches, be on several TV shows, and appear in more than fifty newspapers from coast to coast. The Miracle Walk was over, but the hope that it would bring to millions was only beginning.

Once again God showed me that if I would take care of His business, He would take care of mine!